EscalateEnglish

Student Activity Book

8

Unit 1

CULTURE AND BELONGING

SELECTIONS

BUILD VOCABULARY

Student Activity Book

Escalate English

8

Houghton Mifflin Harcourt

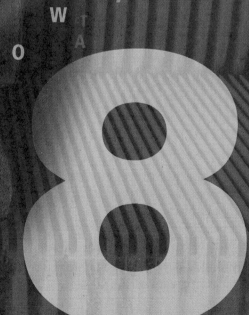

Cover, Title Page Photo Credits: Escalator ©Rodrigo Apolaya/APU Imagenes/Getty Images. All Other Photos ©HMH

HOW ENGLISH WORKS

PERFORMANCE TASK

Unit 2

THE THRILL OF HORROR

SELECTIONS

BUILD VOCABULARY

HOW ENGLISH WORKS

PERFORMANCE TASK

Unit 3

THE MOVE TOWARD FREEDOM

SELECTIONS

BUILD VOCABULARY

HOW ENGLISH WORKS

PERFORMANCE TASK

Unit 4

APPROACHING ADULTHOOD

SELECTIONS

BUILD VOCABULARY

HOW ENGLISH WORKS

PERFORMANCE TASK

Unit 5

PERSONAL LEGACY

SELECTIONS

BUILD VOCABULARY

HOW ENGLISH WORKS

PERFORMANCE TASK

Unit 6

THE VALUE OF WORK

SELECTIONS

BUILD VOCABULARY

HOW ENGLISH WORKS

PERFORMANCE TASK

Table of Contents

Culture and Belonging

"People will not look forward to posterity, who never look backward to their ancestors."

—*Edmund Burke, philosopher*

In what ways did your ancestors influence your culture? What were some of their contributions?

What are some cultural groups you know?

_____

_____

How do people learn about different cultures?

_____

_____

How do cultures change and evolve?

_____

_____

What do you think of when you think of culture?

_____

_____

_____

Academic Vocabulary

As you work through Unit 1, look and listen for these words. Practice using them when you talk in class and in your writing. Write about your experiences using these words in the last column of the chart.

Word	Definition	Related Forms	My Experiences
contribute	• to be a cause of something • to give support	contribution, contributor	
immigrate	to enter and settle in a new country	immigrant, immigration, emigrate	
reaction	a response to something	react	
relocate	to move to a new place	relocation	
shifting	changing or moving	shift	

Unearth a Borrowed Word

To evaluate your speech, use the Presenting a Speech Rubric available from your online Student Resources or from your teacher. Read the Performance Task prompt on Student Book p. 5 before planning your speech.

Plan

1. Plan your speech. Choose your topic.

The example of an English word that has been borrowed from another language is _____.

The original language is _____.

It means _____.

2. Tell about it!

What are the origins of this word?

_____

What is the original meaning of this word?

_____

Why was there a need for this word in English?

_____

3. What sources will you use to look up information about this word?

_____

Use the information on your plan to prepare your speech.

Prepare

A well-organized speech is easier to remember.

1. Make your opening line an attention grabber! What will your opening line be?

_____

_____

2. What are your main points? What information will you include?

_____

_____

3. How will you end your speech?

_____

_____

Draft Your Speech

Use your notes from Activity Book page 3 to write a rough draft of your speech.

You don't have to include every word that you will say, but make sure you have the main points written down so that you can refer to them. Order is important too—write your notes in the order you use in your speech.

Having a complete set of notes will make speaking to your classmates much easier!

_____

_____

_____

_____

_____

_____

_____

_____

_____

_____

_____

_____

_____

_____

_____

_____

_____

_____

_____

_____

_____

_____

_____

_____

_____

_____

How Details Support an Argument

Explore how xgog45 supports the main idea of the argument that California is strange with some details based on cultural differences and others based on occurrences that xgog45 simply finds strange. Cite text evidence to support your ideas.

Details Based on Cultural Differences	Details that xgog45 Simply Finds Strange
_____	_____
_____	_____
_____	_____
_____	_____
_____	_____
_____	_____
_____	_____
_____	_____
_____	_____
_____	_____
_____	_____
_____	_____
_____	_____
_____	_____
_____	_____

Critical Vocabulary

A. Circle four words in the Word Bank that you want to know more about.

Word Bank

confronted	anxious	grizzly bears
shrill	jaywalking	referee

B. Read the selection xgog45 again and look for the words. Complete the activity.

1. Word: _____

What I think it means: _____

What it means: _____

2. Word: _____

What I think it means: _____

What it means: _____

3. Word: _____

What I think it means: _____

What it means: _____

4. Word: _____

What I think it means: _____

What it means: _____

C. Choose three words that you wrote in Part B. Write a sentence using each word.

1. _____

_____

2. _____

_____

3. _____

_____

Write a Blog

To evaluate your blog, use the Blog Rubric available from your online Student Resources or from your teacher.

1. You should be comfortable expressing yourself about the subject of your blog. What will the purpose of your blog be?

_____

_____

_____

_____

2. What website will you use to host your blog? Does your school have one? Have you investigated a free site?

_____

_____

_____

_____

3. What look do you want your blog to have? Have you chosen a title and images for your blog?

_____

_____

_____

_____

Blogging Safety Tips

- Use a nickname when blogging.
- Do not post personal information, such as your last name, address, or the name of your school.
- Remember that whatever you post on the web is permanent.
- Post only positive comments.

Build Vocabulary

Compound Words

A. Circle the correct answer.

1. Which word means "the middle of the day"? (afternoon, after noon)

2. Which word means "straight up, erect"? (up-right, upright)

3. Which word means "an outer side or edge"? (outside, out side)

4. Which word means "a person whose job it is to enforce the law"? (police-officer, police officer)

5. Which means "any person"? (any one, anyone)

| outside | police officer | afternoon | newspaper | goalkeepers |
| upright | anymore | anyone | football | |

B. Complete each sentence with a word from the box.

1. The minute we stepped _____ the bitter cold stung our faces.

2. Even though the field was soaked with rain, our _____ team played a great game.

3. When the national anthem was played, Jose stood _____ and placed his hand over his heart.

4. I don't like playing that game _____ .

5. Francisco was thrilled to learn that the local _____ had covered his role in the team's winning game.

C. Choose five words from the box. Use each word in a sentence.

1. _____

   _____

2. _____

   _____

   _____

3. _____

   _____

4. _____

   _____

5. _____

   _____

Subject, Verb, Object

A. Decide if the underlined word is a subject, verb, object, or none of the above. Circle the correct answer.

1. Josephine rolled her <u>eyes</u>, looking annoyed.

    a. subject   **b.** verb   **c.** object   **d.** none of the above

2. An enormous <u>squid</u> grabbed the fish.

    a. subject   **b.** verb   **c.** object   **d.** none of the above

3. Catalina, the goalie, <u>caught</u> the ball just in time.

    a. subject   **b.** verb   **c.** object   **d.** none of the above

4. <u>Mariel</u> wrote a song for Ian.

    a. subject   **b.** verb   **c.** object   **d.** none of the above

B. Fill in the blank with a word that fits.

1. The juggler tossed white bowling pins and red _____ into the air.

2. _____ and her little brother swim at the beach on Tuesdays.

3. A lot of people _____ for exercise.

4. Joseph _____ as well as his classmates.

5. Diane _____ all of her food for lunch.

C. Choose one topic and write four sentences about it. Use at least two compound subjects and one compound object. Possible topics:

a sister and brother trying to decide how to spend their time	two friends planning what to do over the weekend	two wolves arguing over how to catch prey

1. _____

_____

2. _____

_____

3. _____

_____

4. _____

_____

Sequence

Answer the questions about *Now We Are Cooking!* Write out the step-by-step sequence of the recipe.

1. What is the chef going to cook?

_____

2. What does the chef do first?

_____

3. What ingredients is he using?

_____

4. What does he do next?

_____

5. What is the next step?

_____

6. What happens next?

_____

7. Why does he have to flip the tortilla? _____

Compare and Contrast

Think about the video you have just seen. Compare and contrast it with "xgog45."

1. What common theme do the video and the blog share?

_____

_____

2. How are they different?

_____

_____

_____

3. Which do you think has a more serious tone, the video or the blog? Why?

_____

_____

_____

Critical Vocabulary

A. Circle four words in the Word Bank that you want to know more about.

Word Bank

influence	commute	elements (in a good dish)	handed down	deliciousness
career	authenticity	contribute	whisk	appreciate

B. Watch the video again and listen for the words. Complete the activity.

1. Word: _____

What I think it means: _____

What it means: _____

2. Word: _____

What I think it means: _____

What it means: _____

3. Word: _____

What I think it means: _____

What it means: _____

4. Word: _____

What I think it means: _____

What it means: _____

C. Choose three words that you wrote in Part B. Write a sentence using each word.

1. _____

_____

2. _____

_____

3. _____

_____

Academic Vocabulary

A. Complete each sentence with the correct word from the box.

contribute	contributors	contribution

1. Linda's _____ to the bake sale was her famous oatmeal cookies.

2. The editor of the magazine asked Joanne to _____ articles about holiday recipes.

3. Mr. Kovalev made a large _____ to the library so they could buy new computers.

4. Non-profit organizations must keep a list of their _____ .

B. Read the passage and answer the questions.

> Bill's older brother Sam would like to be on the city council. Even though he is only eighteen, he believes that a young person can contribute ideas for ways to make the city a better place for teenagers. Since he needs money for advertising, he must find some campaign contributors. The law says that each person can make a maximum contribution of $250, so he needs quite a few contributors.

1. What can a young person contribute on the city council?

   _____

2. Sam needs money, so who is he looking for?

   _____

3. How much can each contributor contribute?

   _____

contribute	contribution

C. Using a word from the box, write a sentence about an organization or person you would like to help and the kind of contribution you would like to make.

_____

_____

_____

Critical Vocabulary

A. Read the sentences below. Circle the definition of each underlined word. Remember that you can look up any unfamiliar words in the dictionary.

1. Uncle is <u>pacing</u> around like crazy. *Pacing* means

   a. walking nervously.   **b.** jumping quickly.   **c.** sitting.

2. Sun-hee goes to the <u>cupboard</u> and brings back an old book. *A cupboard is*

   a. a library.   **b.** a storage cabinet.   **c.** a store.

3. I watch him take a few books from the cupboard and turn the pages. Then he gets up again and <u>fetches</u> paper and pencil. *Fetches means*

   a. retrieves and brings back.   **b.** steals.   **c.** borrows.

4. The name chosen by Abuji will <u>honor</u> their family history. *Honor* means

   a. respect.   **b.** build on.   **c.** forget.

B. Choose a word from the box to complete each sentence.

pacing	twist	fetches	clan
register	fortune	honor	cupboard

1. The Campbell _____ gathered for a family reunion.

2. The lawyer might _____ the witness's statement during the trial.

3. We need to _____ our names with the school to attend class.

4. My mother keeps spices in the kitchen _____.

5. Her puppy _____ the ball when it plays.

C. Choose three words from the box in Part B. Use each word in a sentence.

1. _____

_____

2. _____

_____

3. _____

_____

Analyzing Character

Review "Tae-yul" and complete the chart. Provide text evidence of each family member's reaction to the new Japanese rule about names. Write an adjective or phrase describing the character trait that the reaction reveals.

Reaction	Family Member	Character Trait
walks right past me without saying hello	Uncle	irritated

Review the text evidence. Summarize how Abuji's reactions to the new rule show about his role in the family.

_____

_____

_____

_____

_____

Expressions

A. Circle the correct answer.

1. What slang expression means "to be annoying"?

a. a real pain   **b.** like crazy

2. What slang expression means "very intensely"?

a. a real pain   **b.** like crazy

3. What slang expression means "a small child"?

a. a real pain   **b.** kid

4. What slang expression means "what's happening"?

a. what's going on   **b.** way before

real pain	kid	way before	what's going on	like crazy

B. Complete each sentence with a phrase from the box.

1. Enrico ran _____ to make it to his bus on time.

2. _____ supper, Peter was already complaining about how hungry he was.

3. Nothing's ever good enough for Marion. She's a _____.

4. Talk to me and tell me _____.

C. Choose four slang expressions from the box. Use each slang expression in a sentence.

1. _____
_____

2. _____
_____

3. _____
_____

4. _____
_____

Pseudonyms

1. How did Tae-yul's father make the family's new name meaningful?

_____

_____

_____

_____

2. How else could a name be changed to have a "secret" meaning?

_____

_____

_____

_____

3. Describe two methods you could use to come up with a pseudonym you like.

_____

_____

_____

_____

4. Choose a pseudonym for yourself, and explain the method you used to create it.

_____

_____

_____

_____

5. Explain why you like the pseudonym you chose.

_____

_____

_____

_____

Build Vocabulary

Multiple-Meaning Words

The words in the box below are from the selection "Tae-yul." All of the words have multiple meanings.

A. Circle the response that correctly defines the underlined word.

1. Sharon will <u>book</u> an appointment for you with the hairdresser.

   a. schedule   **b.** sheets of printed paper held together by a cover

2. Jose got the lead <u>part</u> in the class play.

   a. some, but not all, of something   **b.** role

3. We were all stiff after <u>sitting</u> for over ten hours on the flight to India.

   a. a period of remaining seated   **b.** the time when a meal is served to a large number of people

4. It was Maria's <u>turn</u> to play tennis.

   a. to move around a central point

   b. an opportunity to do something after other people have done it

5. The class thoroughly enjoyed Mr. Wing's informative <u>talk</u>.

   a. a formal speech or presentation   **b.** to have a conversation with someone

B. Define each underlined word. Remember that you can look up words in the dictionary or online.

1. I always <u>part</u> my hair on the left-hand side. _____

2. <u>Turn</u> around and face the door. _____

3. Manny just loves to <u>talk</u>. _____

4. Paul went online to <u>order</u> a new pair of sneakers. _____

5. Which <u>part</u> of the movie did you like best? _____

C. Choose two words from the box. Use each word in two sentences that show different meanings of the word.

sitting	turn	order	part	talk	book

1. _____

   _____

2. _____

   _____

Subject Verb Object Replaced by Pronoun

A. Choose the correct pronoun to replace the underlined words in the prompt. Circle the correct answer.

1. The Mandan tribe moved to new homes.

   a. They   **b.** You   **c.** He   **d.** She

2. Jessica pole vaults for the track team.

   a. She   **b.** It   **c.** We   **d.** Us

3. I gave gum to Sophia and Maureen.

   a. they   **b.** them   **c.** he   **d.** it

4. Joan and Igor fed bread to the ducks.

   a. he   **b.** them   **c.** they   **d.** her

B. Fill in the blank with a pronoun that fits.

1. Camille likes to lift weights, but _____ hates to run.

2. The Suarez brothers buy me food a lot, and I've never given anything back to _____ .

3. Mrs. Gracie and her husband practice martial arts. In fact, that's how _____ met each other.

4. The cat looked hungry, but we didn't have any food to give _____ .

5. Bob gave me a present, and I gave _____ one in return.

C. Choose one topic and write four sentences about that topic. Use at least two subject pronouns and at least two object pronouns. Possible topics:

people who owe each other favors	how two friends first met each other	a large group making an important decision

1. _____

   _____

2. _____

   _____

3. _____

   _____

4. _____

   _____

Staying on Task

Make notes while reading "Lutefisk and Rømmegrøt: Keeping a Cultural Connection Through Food." Remember, making good notes can help you stay on task.

How well were you able to stay focused as you read the selection?

_____

_____

_____

_____

Did your attention wander? When?

_____

_____

_____

_____

What did you do about it?

_____

_____

_____

_____

What did you do when you came across difficult words?

_____

_____

_____

_____

What helpful tips can you share with your classmates?

_____

_____

_____

_____

Academic Vocabulary

A. Complete each sentence with the correct word from the box.

immigrated	emigrated

1. Jenny _____ to the United States when she was twelve.

immigrating	emigrating

2. If people have relatives in other countries, they sometimes consider _____ from their homelands.

immigrant	immigration

3. Lena had questions about filling out a citizenship application so she called her local _____ office.

immigrants	immigration

4. For some _____, learning English is the biggest challenge.

B. Read the passage and answer the questions.

> Camila works as an immigration officer. She helps immigrants settle into their new country and answers questions about applying for citizenship. Camila enjoys her job because she remembers how lost she felt when she immigrated to the United States twenty years ago. During her vacations, she often travels to Puerto Rico to see her relatives and visit her old neighborhood.

1. What does Camila do as an immigration officer? _____
_____

2. Why does Camila enjoy her job? _____
_____

3. Where did Camila emigrate from twenty years ago? _____
_____

C. Write two sentences about someone who has moved to a new country using the words *immigrate* and *emigrate*.

1. _____
2. _____

Use of Language

Reread "Lutefisk and Rømmegrøt: Keeping a Cultural Connection Through Food."
Think about the ideas the author wants to pass along to the reader and how she keeps
the reader's attention.

Cite text evidence to support your ideas.

What text evidence supports the main idea that traditional Norwegian foods are a part of the Norwegian-American cultural heritage?

What text evidence is a detail that supports the reasons why many Norwegians immigrated to the United States between 1825 and 1925?

What text evidence is a detail that supports the ways Norwegian immigrants keep their traditional culture?

Performance Task

Opinion

What are the advantages of immigrants keeping up the traditions of their native land? What challenges, or difficulties, might be encountered by immigrants who keep up their traditions?

Cite text evidence to support your ideas.

Advantages of Keeping Up Traditions	Text evidence

Challenges Posed by Keeping Up Traditions	Text evidence

Critical Vocabulary

Below are words from "Lutefisk and Rømmegrøt" on pages 17–19 in the Student Book.

A. Circle four words in the Word Bank that you want to know more about.

Word Bank

hardships	ancestral	homeland	relocate
recruits	porridge	mainstream	culinary

B. Read the selection again and look for the words. Write what you think each word means. Next, look the words up in the dictionary and write down the meanings. See how close your meaning comes to the dictionary meaning.

1. Word: _____

What I think it means: _____

What it means: _____

2. Word: _____

What I think it means: _____

What it means: _____

3. Word: _____

What I think it means: _____

What it means: _____

4. Word: _____

What I think it means: _____

What it means: _____

C. Choose three words that you wrote in Part B. Write a sentence using each word.

1. _____

_____

2. _____

_____

3. _____

_____

Create a Compare/Contrast Chart

As you listen to the podcast, write about why certain words and phrases are expressed one way in English and another way in Pirahã. Place one detail in each box.

How It Is Expressed in English	How It Is Expressed in Pirahã	Reasons for Difference
words	words, humming, whistling	_____ _____ _____ _____ _____
"I'll see you in six months."	"I'll see you when the water reaches this point on the bank."	_____ _____ _____ _____ _____
"He caught a fish."	"He caught a fish (I know because I saw him do it)."	_____ _____ _____ _____ _____
"John's brother's house"	"John has a brother. This brother has a house."	_____ _____ _____ _____ _____

Critical Vocabulary

A. Read the sentences below. Circle the definition of each underlined word. Remember that you can look up any unfamiliar words in the dictionary.

1. In the podcast you'll listen to next, one man has to <u>adapt</u> when he starts living with a group of people whose language is very different from his own. *Adapt* means

    a. adjust.   **b.** neglect.   **c.** refuse.

2. The Pirahã were first contacted in the 1700s, but have remained mostly <u>isolated</u> from the rest of the world. *Isolated* means

    a. separated.   **b.** together.   **c.** ignored.

3. The Pirahã language is of great interest to <u>linguists</u> like Daniel Everett. A *linguist* is

    a. someone who studies rhythm.   **b.** someone who studies cultures.
    c. someone who studies language.

4. In Pirahã, phrases cannot be <u>embedded</u> in other phrases. *Embedded* means

    a. enclosed.   **b.** spoken.   **c.** written.

B. Choose a word from the box to complete each sentence.

adapt	isolated	linguists	embedded
cycle	rhthym	tone	features

1. Someone's _____ of voice will tell you if he is happy or sad.

2. Many cultures will understand time by noting the _____ of the river or moon.

3. As I listened to the rise and fall of the Pirahã's voices, I realized they had a unique _____ to their language.

4. A person may feel _____ if they do not know the local language.

5. Linguists study the different _____ found across the world's many languages.

C. Choose three words from the box in Part B. Use each word in a sentence.

1. _____

_____

2. _____

_____

3. _____

_____

Podcast: "Daniel Everett on Language"

Collaborative Discussion Support

How are the English and Pirahã Languages similar to each other? How are they different? Discuss your ideas with a partner.

Ways English and Pirahã Are Similar
_____
_____
_____

Ways English and Pirahã Are Different
_____
_____
_____

Write a description for something without using color or number words. Then, read your description to a partner.

_____

_____

_____

_____

_____

Discuss with a partner why you think it would be useful or not to tell exactly how you know something when you are talking to that person.

_____

_____

_____

_____

_____

Specialized Vocabulary

concept	linguistic	tone	syntax	culture

A. Choose the correct word from the box to answer each question.

1. Which word describes the way in which words are put together in phrases, clauses, and sentences?
_____

2. Which word means "an idea"? _____

3. Which word means "relating to languages"? _____

4. Which word means "the beliefs, customs, and art of a particular group of people"?
_____

5. Which word means "the quality of a person's voice, including its rhythm, pitch, and loudness"?
_____

B. Complete each sentence with the correct word from the box.

concept	linguistic	pitch	syntax	culture

1. As a _____ expert, Adele had devoted her life to the study of languages.

2. The ancient Mayans had a highly advanced civilization and _____.

3. Brian's _____ was to retell the story using dialogue and music.

4. The poet's _____, or arrangement of words, is quite unusual.

5. The _____ of her voice was high and very shrill.

C. Choose three words from the box in Part B. Use each word in a sentence.

1. _____

_____

2. _____

_____

3. _____

_____

Verbs Tenses

A. Identify the tense of the underlined word. Circle the correct answer.

1. The history teacher <u>showed</u> us an ancient painting yesterday.

   a. past   **b.** present   **c.** future   **d.** none of the above

2. The museum guide <u>explains</u> the exhibits to visitors.

   a. past   **b.** present   **c.** future   **d.** none of the above

3. Serafina <u>tells</u> me that making a simple website is pretty easy.

   a. past   **b.** present   **c.** future   **d.** none of the above

4. Mr. Coates's presentation <u>will show</u> how to research a social science paper.

   a. past   **b.** present   **c.** future   **d.** none of the above

B. Fill in the blank with a word in the appropriate tense.

1. Tyrone _____ breakfast yesterday morning.

2. Mrs. Yang _____ at the meeting tomorrow.

3. Josie _____ every day.

4. My friend from the Philippines _____ about home a lot.

5. Most scientists thought this wasn't possible, but last year Dr. Banner _____ that it was possible.

C. Choose one topic and write four sentences about it. Use at least one past, one present, and one future tense verb. Possible topics:

a skill that someone practices	playing your favorite game	how you get to school and how you get home

1. _____

   _____

2. _____

   _____

3. _____

   _____

4. _____

   _____

Critical Vocabulary

A. Read the sentences below. Circle the definition of each underlined word. Remember that you can look up any unfamiliar words in the dictionary.

1. A man named Edward Sheriff Curtis set out to provide <u>documentation</u> of the vanishing cultures of the American West. *Documentation* means

   a. records.   **b.** a list.   **c.** contracts.

2. His skill and <u>charisma</u> resulted in his being invited as official photographer on an expedition to explore Alaska. *Charisma* means

   a. unpleasantness.   **b.** charm.   **c.** intelligence.

3. The photographer was a genius, and his subjects possessed unusual strength, beauty, and <u>dignity</u>. *Dignity* means

   a. quality of being worthy of respect.   **b.** quality of having wealth.   **c.** having many relatives.

4. Curtis photographed <u>scenic</u> views of Mount Rainier. *Scenic* means

   a. black and white.   **b.** dangerous.   **c.** beautiful.

B. Choose a word from the box to complete each sentence.

documentation	scenic	charisma	expedition
dignity	masterpiece	dissolving	studio

1. Photographs are a form of visual _____.

2. At the turn of the twentieth-century, Native American cultures were in danger of _____.

3. Curtis's photographs were developed in his photography _____.

4. The west coast of America contains many _____ views.

5. An _____ across the country takes time and effort.

C. Choose three words from the box in Part B. Use each word in a sentence.

1. _____

2. _____

3. _____

Academic Vocabulary

A. Complete each sentence with the correct word from the box.

reacted	reacting

1. Marielle _____ to the cat on her doorstep by picking it up and petting it.

reactions	reaction

2. Jamie doesn't drink milk because he has an allergic _____ to dairy products.

reacted	reaction

3. Hydrogen cars run on electricity produced by a chemical _____.

reacted	reacting

4. Stanley showed his friends how a carbonated drink _____ with a mint candy to create carbon dioxide foam.

react	reacted	reaction

B. Rewrite each sentence using one of the words from the box.

1. When Tim saw the grade on his math test.

_____

2. When the cat jumped from the tree and landed in front of the dog.

_____

C. Using one of the words from the box, write a sentence about the last time you were surprised about something.

_____

_____

_____

Impact of Author's Style

Examine the text to see how the author has presented facts in a way that has an impact on the reader.

Give examples from the text that present facts in a strong, effective way.

_____

_____

_____

_____

_____

_____

_____

Give examples from the text in which the author uses verbs and adjectives effectively.

_____

_____

_____

_____

_____

_____

_____

Build Vocabulary

Greek Roots

Many English words contain roots that come from older languages, such as Greek and Latin. Knowing the meaning of the word's root can help you determine the word's meaning.

charisma	democracy	biology	chronic	chronological
biography	charismatic	democratic	monologue	monocle

A. Write the word from the box to answer each question.

1. Which word means "in time order"? _____

2. Which word means "the story of someone's life"? _____

3. Which word means "long lasting"? _____

4. Which word describes someone who has a special charm or appeal? _____

5. Which word means "a form of government in which people choose their leaders by voting"?

_____

B. Complete each sentence with a word from the box.

1. In order to complete the assignment, Bing had to put the events in _____ order.

2. In _____ class we studied photosynthesis.

3. The actor's fifteen-minute _____ was extraordinarily moving.

4. A _____ illness is an illness that lasts for a long time.

5. Tom had a ridiculous looking _____ on his left eye.

C. Choose three words from the box. Use each word in a sentence.

1. _____
   _____
   _____

2. _____
   _____
   _____

3. _____
   _____
   _____

Build Vocabulary

Homophones

A. Circle the correct homophone.

1. Which word means "achieved victory or success"?

   a. one   **b.** won

2. Which word means "to find out how heavy someone or something is"?

   a. weigh   **b.** way

3. Which word means "periods of 24 hours"?

   a. days   **b.** daze

4. Which word means "the repetition of something to be memorized or learned"?

   a. rote   **b.** wrote

5. Which word means "to perform or execute"?

   a. do   **b.** due

B. Complete each sentence with the correct homophone.

1. After being hit on the head, Martina was in a _____. (days, daze)

2. You have to _____ your homework before you can play video games. (do, due)

3. Martin is going to _____ his leather jacket to the game. (where, wear)

4. Your science assignment is _____ on Thursday. (do, due)

5. I have my own _____ of making spaghetti sauce. (way, weigh)

C. Choose three homophone sets from the box. Use each word in a sentence that shows the difference in meaning and spelling between the two words.

do/due	way/weigh	one/won	days/daze	where/wear	wrote/rote

1. homophones: _____ and _____

   _____

   _____

2. homophones: _____ and _____

   _____

   _____

3. homophones: _____ and _____

   _____

   _____

Build Vocabulary

Critical Vocabulary

A. Read the sentences below. Circle the definition of each underlined word. Remember that you can look up any unfamiliar words in the dictionary.

1. Twins may use similar <u>strategies</u> when they play games. *Strategies* are

   a. plans   **b.** behaviors.   **c.** cheats.

2. He or she is an <u>individual</u> who is different from any other person. An *individual* is a

   a. twin.   **b.** single person.   **c.** sibling.

3. Twins may <u>develop</u> at similar rates. To *develop* means to

   a. grow.   **b.** forget.   **c.** play.

4. A <u>mutation</u> may cause one twin to be slightly different from the other. A *mutation* is

   a. a change in form.   **b.** a copy.   **c.** a fraternal twin.

B. Choose a word from the box to complete each sentence.

mutations	gender	cooperate	develop
perspective	individual	strategies	effortlessly

1. Twins or close siblings often communicate _____ with each other.

2. Siblings can learn to _____ with each other, despite minor disagreements.

3. Identical twins come from a common _____ that occurs after a fertilized egg splits.

4. I never share the same _____ and opinion as my sister.

5. Identical twins are usually the same _____ .

C. Choose three words from the box in Part B. Use each word in a sentence.

1. _____

   _____

2. _____

   _____

3. _____

   _____

Choose the Correct Progressive Tense

A. Decide if the underlined word is in the past progressive, present progressive, or future progressive tense. Circle the correct answer.

1. Look out, that tree <u>is falling</u> down!

    a. past progressive   **b.** present progressive   **c.** future progressive   **d.** none of the above

2. Jocelyn <u>writes</u> unfair questions sometimes.

    a. past progressive   **b.** present progressive   **c.** future progressive   **d.** none of the above

3. Pablo's father <u>will be teaching</u> me how to fish next month.

    a. past progressive   **b.** present progressive   **c.** future progressive   **d.** none of the above

4. Imelda <u>was arguing</u> with the cashier over how much eggs cost.

    a. past progressive   **b.** present progressive   **c.** future progressive   **d.** none of the above

B. Complete each sentence with a <u>progressive verb</u> that fits.

1. Nick _____ to catch the bus, but I don't think he'll get there in time.

2. If he doesn't catch the bus, he _____ home tonight.

3. The bus _____ slowly, though, so he has a chance.

4. The old farmer _____ that it would rain, and he was right.

5. Somewhere, an airplane _____ right now.

C. Choose one topic and write four sentences about that topic. Use at least three progressive tense verbs. Possible topics:

learning how to do something you're interested in	what someone who was sitting in a library all day did	an exciting visitor arriving at school

1. _____

    _____

2. _____

    _____

3. _____

    _____

4. _____

    _____

Collaborative Discussion Support

Look through "Small Cultures." Find information to complete the graphic organizer. Write one or more examples in each box for text evidence.

Main Idea
_____
_____
_____
_____

Text Evidence
_____
_____
_____
_____
_____
_____
_____

Text Evidence
_____
_____
_____
_____
_____
_____
_____

Text Evidence
_____
_____
_____
_____
_____
_____
_____

Conclusion
_____
_____

Academic Vocabulary

relocated	relocation

A. Complete each sentence with the correct word from the box.

1. After the Greenbergs retired, they _____ to Maine to be closer to their grandchildren.

2. After Town Diner's _____ to the university district, it had many more customers.

B. Read the passage and answer the questions.

> Mr. Williams has lived on the third floor of Mrs. Landry's house for many years. Mrs. Landry is planning to move out of the country, so she has offered to relocate him to an apartment building. Mr. Williams is getting older and likes the idea of relocating to a building with an elevator, especially if Mrs. Landry will help him with his relocation.

1. Why does Mr. Williams need to relocate?

   He needs to relocate because Mrs. Landry _____.

2. What has Mrs. Landry offered to do?

   She has offered _____.

3. Why does Mr. Williams like the idea of relocation?

   He likes the idea of relocation because the new building will have _____.

C. Using *relocate* or *relocation*, write a sentence about where you would live if you could relocate to any place in the world.

_____

_____

_____

_____

_____

_____

_____

_____

_____

Build Vocabulary

Critical Vocabulary

A. Read the sentences below. Circle the definition of each underlined word. Remember that you can look up any unfamiliar words in the dictionary.

1. Many <u>merchants</u> sold goods along The Silk Road. *Merchants* are

   a. criminals.   **b.** lawyers   **c.** traders.

2. Warring countries may draw a <u>truce</u> if they want to end the war. A *truce* is

   a. a form of warfare.   **b.** an agreement to stop fighting.   **c.** a battle

2. Ancient China's greatest <u>export</u> was silk. An *export* is

   a. a product sold abroad.   **b.** a popular item.   **c.** a product brought from abroad.

3. Marco Polo found life back in Italy <u>dreary</u> after his travels. *Dreary* means

   a. dull.   **b.** exciting.   **c.** rigorous.

4. The <u>splendor</u> of Kublai Khan's court impressed Marco Polo. *Splendor* means

   a. ugliness.   **b.** magnificence.   **c.** strangeness.

B. Choose a word from the box to complete each sentence.

merchant	export	curious	ambassadors
impressions	dreary	truce	splendor

1. _____ represent their own country or religion on travels abroad.

2. Marco Polo's adventures made people _____ about life outside of Venice.

3. The exotic cultures Marco Polo encountered were full of beauty and _____.

4. Travelers may write their _____ of their adventures in a travel diary.

5. After getting the travel bug, normal life might seem _____ to those used to taking vacations abroad.

C. Choose three words from the box in Part B. Use each word in a sentence.

1. _____

   _____

2. _____

   _____

3. _____

   _____

Specialized Vocabulary

explorers	traded	posts	route
export	expedition	safe passage	

A. Write the correct word from the box to answer each question.

1. Which word means "people who travel to faraway places in search of new information"?

   _____

2. Which word means "bought, sold, and exchanged goods or services"? _____

3. Which word means "to carry or send a product from one place to another"? _____

4. Which word means "protection offered to someone who is travelling and might be in danger"?

   _____

5. Which word means "a group of people who travel together to a distant place"?

   _____

B. Complete each sentence with the correct word from the box.

1. _____ had always fascinated Kim because they are so brave and so curious.

2. What _____ do you plan to take to get from the school to the concert hall?

3. The government had offered us _____ into the country.

4. The company decided to _____ its products to Brazil.

5. The _____ includes twenty people and is scheduled to last for two months.

C. Choose three words from the box. Use each word in a sentence.

1. _____

   _____

   _____

2. _____

   _____

   _____

3. _____

   _____

   _____

Collaborative Discussion Support

Marco Polo

Work with a partner. Discuss your impressions of Marco Polo. Cite text evidence to support your ideas.

You will use your notes from the graphic organizer below to write your paragraph.

Was Marco Polo intelligent?

My impressions	Text Evidence

Was Marco Polo sensible?

My impressions	Text Evidence

Was Marco Polo naturally adventurous?

My impressions	Text Evidence

Did Marco Polo get along with others?

My impressions	Text Evidence

The Prefixes *ex–* and *pre–*

previous	precognition	expedition	exhaust
precede	predawn	excel	exile

A. Choose a word from the box to answer each question.

1. Which word means "to come before"? _____

2. Which word means "occurring beforehand"? _____

3. Which word means "to surpass? _____

4. Which word means "to remove from a country"? _____

5. Which word means "to drain or to tire out"? _____

B. Complete each sentence with a word from the box at the top of the page.

1. She couldn't explain it, but Adele had a _____ that something bad was about to happen.

2. Starting the trip at _____ is a good idea because it means we will miss any chance of heavy traffic.

3. The _____ performer will be a very hard act to follow.

4. The _____ to Antarctica will include 30 people and last for three months.

5. Frank was determined to _____ in math.

C. Choose three words from the box at the top of the page. Use each word in a sentence.

1. _____
_____
_____

2. _____
_____
_____

3. _____
_____
_____

Verbs in the Perfect Tense

A. Decide if the underlined word is in the past perfect, present perfect, or future perfect tense. Circle the correct answer.

1. Margaret <u>has defeated</u> two opponents so far.

   a. past perfect   **b.** present perfect   **c.** future perfect   **d.** none of the above

2. Mitchell <u>had asked</u> three friends for help before he found one who could help him.

   a. past perfect   **b.** present perfect   **c.** future perfect   **d.** none of the above

3. Elodie is tired, because she <u>has worked</u> very hard today.

   a. past perfect   **b.** present perfect   **c.** future perfect   **d.** none of the above

4. Boris <u>will have finished</u> his robot by tomorrow afternoon.

   a. past perfect   **b.** present perfect   **c.** future perfect   **d.** none of the above

B. Complete each sentence with a <u>perfect tense verb</u> that fits.

1. That computer is no good—it _____ three times so far!

2. Keisha _____ her phone, so I helped her find it.

3. The dog _____ its food by the time we get back.

4. Omar _____ the problem, but he refused to tell anyone else the solution.

5. The Fang sisters _____ that they were at the party, but no one saw them.

C. Choose one topic and write four sentences about that topic. Use at least three perfect tense verbs. Possible topics:

several surprising events happening in a row	a friend making a promise and keeping it	someone describing exciting things they have seen

1. _____

   _____

2. _____

   _____

3. _____

   _____

4. _____

   _____

Speaking Activity: Discussion

Work with your group. Discuss the things you might miss if you were to be away from your neighborhood or country for a long period of time.

Concrete Items	Abstract Assets
_____	_____
_____	_____
_____	_____
_____	_____
_____	_____
_____	_____
_____	_____
_____	_____
_____	_____

People	Where You Are When You're Not Here
_____	_____
_____	_____
_____	_____
_____	_____
_____	_____
_____	_____
_____	_____
_____	_____
_____	_____

Visual Clues

trading	route	tablet	impressions	curious

A. Choose the correct answer from the words in the box.

1. Which word means "a way to get from one place to another"? _____

2. Which word means "buying and selling goods or products"? _____

3. Which word means "eager to know or learn something"? _____

4. Which word means "ideas or feelings about something"? _____

5. Which word means "a flat slab of stone, clay, or wood meant to be written on"? _____

B. Match a word from the box to each description of an illustration below. The word you choose should be a definition of what's going on in the description.

1. A man steering a boat with packages on it; in the background buildings and people standing in

   front of them _____

2. A red line on a map that shows "The Silk Road" _____

3. A man showing a bright rectangular object to a group of people _____

4. Marco Polo observing a group of people in front of him and writing down what he sees

   _____

5. Marco Polo talking to Kublai Khan; Kublai Khan listening intently _____

C. Choose three words from the box at the top of the page. Use each word in a sentence that is <u>not</u> about Marco Polo and his adventures.

1. _____

   _____

2. _____

   _____

3. _____

   _____

Performance Task

Write Down Possible Questions

You will be writing an essay that analyzes the literary elements in "When My Name Was Keoko." Write down any questions that might help you decide on a main topic for your literary analysis.

Questions about Character

_____

_____

_____

_____

Questions about Dialogue

_____

_____

_____

_____

Questions about Tone

_____

_____

_____

_____

Questions about Setting

_____

_____

_____

_____

Other Questions

_____

_____

_____

_____

Identify Style Elements

Answer the questions below to help with your literary analysis of "When My Name Was Keoko." To evaluate ideas for your essay, use the Literary Analysis Rubric available from your online Student Resources or from your teacher.

Theme

1. How does the author communicate the theme of culture and belonging?

_____

_____

_____

Setting

2. How does the setting contribute to the story? [Hint: setting includes more than just place and time. It also includes the period in which the story is set and cultural influences such as dress, speech, and customs.]

_____

_____

_____

3. What are some specific details about setting that you can use to support your main idea?

_____

_____

_____

Setting

4. What details suggest the mood and tone of the story?

_____

_____

Word Choice and Point of View

5. How does the author use word choice and point of view to emphasize important ideas? (write down examples)

_____

_____

_____

_____

Academic Vocabulary

A. Choose the best description of the type of *shift* indicated in the sentence and circle the answer.

1. The on-off switch on the radio sometimes shifts to "off" by itself because of a manufacturing defect.

   a. something moves   **b.** a change in direction   **c.** workers

2. When the rain finally stopped, there was a major shift in the students' mood.

   a. something moves   **b.** a change in direction   **c.** work schedule

3. Paula works the morning shift at a coffee shop, so she has keys to unlock the door.

   a. something moves   **b.** a change in direction   **c.** work schedule

B. Complete the answers with information from the text.

> The comedian likes to shift between jokes that make you laugh and ones that make you groan. Many of her jokes show how a shift in tone can change the meaning of a sentence. She sometimes jokes about funny things that happened when she worked the night shift as a college student.

1. What does the comedian shift between?

   She likes to shift _____.

2. How does she play with the tone in her sentences?

   She shows how a _____.

3. What shift did she work when she was a college student?

   She worked _____.

C. Using *shift* or *shifting*, write a sentence about the way your attitude towards something has changed over the years.

_____

_____

_____

_____

Finalize Your Plan

WRITING TOOLBOX

Elements of a Literary Analysis

Introduction	"Hook" your audience with an interesting detail, question, or quotation that relates to your main idea. Identify what you will be describing, and state your controlling idea.
Main Idea and Details	Follow a framework to organize your main ideas and supporting evidence. You may choose to use a paragraph for each main idea and its supporting details. Include relevant facts, concrete details, and other text evidence. Restate your ideas.
Conclusion	Summarize the key points and restate your controlling idea. Include an insight that follows from and supports your controlling idea.

A. Review the elements of a literary analysis above. Describe the elements that you will include in your essay.

Introduction _____

_____

_____

Main Idea and Details _____

_____

_____

Conclusion _____

_____

_____

B. Write a brief summary of your analysis.

_____

_____

_____

_____

Vocabulary Review

Here are some of the words you learned in this unit. Choose words from this list and sort them into categories below. There are many possible correct answers! Also, many of the words fit into more than one category.

adapt	culture	emigrated	precognition
afternoon	cycle	immigrant	react
anymore	democracy	impressions	register
biography	democratic	isolated	rhythm
biology	develop	linguistic	splendor
book	dreary	linguists	syntax
charisma	effortlessly	monocle	talk
charismatic	embedded	monologue	tone
chronic	exhaust	newspaper	truce
chronological	expedition	order	turn
contribute	features	outside	upright
contribution	football	part	
cooperate	goalkeepers	perspective	

Words with Greek Prefixes or Roots

1. _____
2. _____
3. _____
4. _____

Specialized Vocabulary about Language

1. _____
2. _____
3. _____
4. _____

Compound Words

1. _____
2. _____
3. _____
4. _____

Multiple-Meaning Words

1. Word: _____

   Definition 1: _____

   Definition 2: _____

2. Word: _____

   Definition 1: _____

   Definition 2: _____

Easily Confused Words

A. Decide which word best completes the sentence. Circle the correct answer.

1. The _____ left to look for new opportunities

   a. emigrant   **b.** immigrant   **c.** there   **d.** they're

2. The mechanics are very good at _____ jobs.

   a. there   **b.** their   **c.** they're   **d.** emigrant

3. Salman is an _____ who came here from Bangladesh.

   a. emigrant   **b.** immigrant   **c.** their   **d.** they're

4. I don't know where those people are going, but _____ sure going fast.

   a. emigrant   **b.** their   **c.** there   **d.** they're

B. Fill in the blank with a word that fits from one of the following: *emigrant, immigrant, there, they're,* or *their.*

1. _____ is a bus parked outside.

2. The brothers left _____ shoes at the beach.

3. Yin is an _____ who arrived in this city just yesterday.

4. The firefighters told me that _____ going to put out a warehouse fire downtown.

5. I'm not certain where Marcus and Daniel are, but I think _____ upstairs.

C. Choose one topic and write four sentences about that topic. Use either *immigrant* or *emigrant* at least once, and use at least two of *there, their,* or *they're*. Possible topics:

how one family came to America	*why* a family decided to leave their home country and come to America	advice you would give to people newly arriving in America

1. _____

   _____

2. _____

   _____

3. _____

   _____

4. _____

   _____

The Thrill of Horror

"Where there is no imagination, there is no horror."

—Arthur Conan Doyle, author

What comes to your mind when you think of horror? You can make visual notes or write.

Why do you think this unit is titled "The Thrill of Horror"? What is thrilling about horror?

What kinds of things are scariest to you?

Do you think other people are scared by the same things that scare you? Why or why not?

Do you like to be scared? If so, what kind of "scary" do you enjoy?

Other notes about horror and scary things

Academic Vocabulary

As you work through Unit 2, look and listen for these words. Practice using them when you talk in class and in your writing. Write about your experiences using these words in the last column of the chart.

Word	Definition	Related Forms	My Experiences
convention	• a custom that is widely accepted and followed • a large meeting where people discuss shared interests	conventional, unconventional	
predict	to say that something will happen in the future	prediction, predictable, unpredictable	
psychology	• the science or study of the mind and behavior • the way a person or group thinks	psychological, psychologist	
summary	a short description of the main points	summarize	
technique	a way of doing something by using special knowledge or skill	technical, technically	

Shades of Meaning

Write a sentence that uses each word below. Pay attention to the different meanings of these adjectives. If you are unsure of the precise definitions of each adjective, check a dictionary. For number 6, choose an adjective that describes someone who is scared and write a sentence for it.

1. anxious

_____

_____

_____

2. startled

_____

_____

_____

3. unnerved

_____

_____

_____

4. scared

_____

_____

_____

5. terrified

_____

_____

_____

6. My word: _____

_____

_____

_____

Scary Situation Paragraph

To evaluate your paragraph, use the Narrative Writing Rubric available from your online Student Resources or from your teacher.

Plan

1. Work with your partner to choose a scary situation. Use your imaginations, but be respectful of your classmates and teacher. **Browse** magazine offers more suggestions to help you brainstorm.

   The scary situation we chose is _____

   _____

2. Decide whether to write your paragraph in first or third person.

   _____

3. What happens in this situation? Identify the setting, including the time and place. List the events in order. Remember that you are writing just one paragraph.

   _____

4. How can you make this situation really scary? Think about appealing to your readers' senses of sight, hearing, touch, and smell. Get their imaginations going!

   _____

Draft

1. Start with a sentence that will get readers' attention. What will make them want to keep reading?

   _____

   _____

2. Tell readers what happens next, including what the main character/narrator is thinking and feeling.

   _____

   _____

3. How will you end your paragraph? Will you tell readers what was really happening, or will you let them use their imaginations?

   _____

   _____

4. Now work together to rewrite your paragraph, checking grammar and spelling and maybe adding another scary detail.

   _____

   _____

Collaborative Discussion Support

Reread the blog "Off the Top of My Head" in the Student Book. Answer the questions below.

Discussing the Purpose

What words and phrases help create a scary mood in this blog?

_____

_____

_____

Point of View

Identify the point of view used by the blogger. (Is the blog written in the first person, the second person, or third person?) Why is the blog written from that point of view?

_____

_____

_____

How would the blog change if it were told from another point of view?

_____

_____

_____

Staying Safe

Why is it important to avoid identifying yourself in a blog?

_____

_____

_____

What kinds of information should you never include?

_____

_____

_____

Use your answers for the Collaborative Discussion on **Student Book** page 54.

© Houghton Mifflin Harcourt Publishing Company

Critical Vocabulary

A. Read the sentences below. Circle the definition of each underlined word. Remember that you can look up any unfamiliar words in the dictionary.

1. My friend Maria sketches ghosts and goblins in her notebook. *Sketches* means

   a. makes rough drawings.   **b.** writes about.   **c.** creates sculptures.

2. The little boy vowed to get revenge on the monster who had stolen his toys. *Revenge* is

   a. sympathy.   **b.** payback.   **c.** forgiveness.

3. The bat made a terrible screeching noises at night that hurt our ears. *Screeching* means

   a. a high-pitched shriek.   **b.** a low whisper.   **c.** a heavy murmur.

4. We are lost and wandering in the middle of a forest. *Wandering* means

   a. walking quickly.   **b.** skipping.   **c.** walking without a known destination.

B. Choose a word from the box to complete each sentence.

sketches	spooky	menacing	furious
distracted	wandering	screeching	revenge

1. I was _____ that my mother frightened me in front of my friends.

2. The man wanted to seek _____ on the prankster that had damaged his yard.

3. It is easy to get _____ by trick or treating when doing your homework on Halloween.

4. The monster peered in the window and showed a _____ snarl.

5. I wasn't sure if my black cat costume was _____ enough for the Halloween party.

C. Choose three words from the box in Part B. Use each word in a sentence.

1. _____

   _____

2. _____

   _____

3. _____

   _____

Writing Activity: Brainstorm Topics for Your Blog

To evaluate your blog, use the Blog Rubric available from your online Student Resources or from your teacher.

1. Choose the next topic for your blog. The suggestions on **Student Book** page 55 might give you some ideas. Also think about current issues at school or in your community. Are school officials thinking about lengthening the school day? Are school uniforms being considered? Might "snow days" be cut? Is a new mall being planned? Does your community need a new park or a community center? What's going on that you care about? The topic I will write about next is

   _____

   _____

   _____

2. Why is this topic interesting to you? Why will it interest your readers?

   _____

   _____

   _____

3. What main points will you include in this blog? Don't try to cover them all! Focus on one or two main points, along with supporting details. You can cover more in your next blogs. In addition, feedback from your readers will tell you what interests them.

   _____

   _____

   _____

4. What sources will you check for information on your topic?

   _____

   _____

   _____

5. What files or links might you include in your blog?

   _____

   _____

   _____

6. How will you end your blog? Will you encourage others to comment on it?

   _____

   _____

   _____

Onomatopoeia

A. Circle the correct answer.

1. Which is an example of when someone might be *whispering*?

    a. when the person is telling someone else a secret

    b. when the person is talking to someone on the other side of the room

2. Which animal makes a *hissing* sound?

    a. a snake   **b.** a horse

3. Which thing might be *rattling* in a strong wind?

    a. curtains   **b.** windows

4. Which thing makes a *blowing* noise?

    a. rain   **b.** wind

rattling	scratching	whispering	thumping
hissing	screeching	blowing	

B. Complete each sentence with a word from the box.

1. Frank failed the test because he got caught _____ an answer to a friend.

2. The large truck finally came to a _____ halt.

3. The _____ cat reared up, ready to attack at a moment's notice.

4. The song has great guitar riffs backed up by a _____ bass beat.

5. The windows in our old house were all _____ in the howling wind.

C. Choose four words from the box. Use each word in a sentence.

1. _____

_____

2. _____

_____

3. _____

_____

4. _____

_____

Gerunds as Subjects and Subject Complements

A. Decide which word in each sentence is the gerund. Circle the correct answer.

1. Exercising regularly takes a lot of self-control.

    a. takes   **b.** exercising   **c.** self-control   **d.** regularly

2. One of my favorite pastimes is reading comics.

    a. reading   **b.** favorite   **c.** one   **d.** is

3. Dancing can be intimidating, but it's also a lot of fun.

    a. intimidating   **b.** it's   **c.** but   **d.** dancing

4. The worst part of an annual check-up is waiting for the doctor.

    a. annual   **b.** worst   **c.** waiting   **d.** of

B. Complete each sentence with a gerund.

1. My favorite part of this movie is the _____.

2. _____ my phone takes forever.

3. _____ slowly helped Kiera calm down.

4. The sound I heard was _____.

5. _____ notes requires me to have at least one hand free.

C. Choose one topic and write four sentences about it. Include at least one gerund as a subject and at least one gerund as a subject complement in your paragraph. Possible topics:

describe the best day of your life	pick a fictional character you'd like to meet and explain why	describe a goal you have

1. _____

    _____

2. _____

    _____

3. _____

    _____

4. _____

    _____

Gathering Information

Answer the questions about *That's Horrific!*

1. What is the kids' assignment?

_____

2. What did Leah do to get ready for the assignment?

_____

3. Why are the kids at Emily's studio?

_____

4. What do they ask Emily?

_____

5. What do they suggest the special effects make-up should be?

_____

6. What do the kids do while Emily works?

_____

7. What is the end result of Emily's work?

_____

Compare And Contrast

Think about the video you have just seen. Compare and contrast it with "Off the Top of My Head."

1. What common theme do the video and the blog share?

_____

_____

_____

2. What similar feeling do the kids in the video and the author of the blog experience?

_____

_____

_____

3. How are the video and the blog different?

_____

_____

_____

Critical Vocabulary

A. Circle four words in the Word Bank that you want to know more about.

Word Bank

mental	apprehension	horrifying	witnessing	situation	incorporate	zombies
supernatural	oozing	techniques	unsettling	conventions	airbrushes	

B. Watch the video *That's Horrific!* again and listen for the words. Complete the activity.

1. Word: _____

What I think it means: _____

What it means: _____

2. Word: _____

What I think it means: _____

What it means: _____

3. Word: _____

What I think it means: _____

What it means: _____

4. Word: _____

What I think it means: _____

What it means: _____

C. Choose three words that you wrote in Part B. Write a sentence using each word.

1. _____

_____

2. _____

_____

3. _____

_____

Academic Vocabulary

A. Decide if each statement describes a conventional or unconventional situation, and complete the chart by writing the correct word.

Situation	Conventional/Unconventional
taking a limousine to school	
a science fiction story with an alien in it	
traveling by hot air balloon	
a house painted bright pink	
a car powered by gasoline	

B. Complete the answers with information from the text.

> When the newspaper started an interactive website with blogs, it was an unconventional idea. But these days, it would be conventional since more people read websites and blogs than printed newspapers. For decades, newspapers followed certain journalistic conventions, but many of those conventions have changed in the twenty-first century.

1. When the newspaper started a website with blogs, what kind of idea was it?

It was _____

_____.

2. Why would it be a conventional idea now?

It would be conventional because now _____

_____.

3. What has happened to the journalistic conventions newspapers followed?

In the twenty-first century _____

_____.

C. Complete the sentences.

1. One of the conventions of detective fiction is _____

_____

2. When I feel like being unconventional, I _____

_____

Critical Vocabulary

A. Read the sentences below. Circle the definition of each underlined word. Remember that you can look up any unfamiliar words in the dictionary.

1. Visiting a haunted house can be an <u>exhilarating</u> experience. *Exhilarating* means

   a. sickening.   **b.** exciting.   **c.** expensive.

2. Getting surprised when you least expect it can <u>trigger</u> an extreme response. *Trigger* means

   a. like.   **b.** pretend.   **c.** set off.

3. When trying to escape the maze, I felt the blood <u>coursing</u> through my veins. *Coursing* means

   a. running through.   **b.** heating up.   **c.** running cold.

4. I feel very <u>alert</u> when walking through a dark and spooky haunted house. *Alert* means

   a. silly.   **b.** afraid.   **c.** aware.

B. Choose a word from the box to complete each sentence.

exhilarating	unscathed	alert	genuine
trigger	sensitive	thrill	coursing

1. The noises coming from the basement made us stand _____.

2. I left the haunted house safe and completely _____.

3. We are such _____ fans of horror movies that we watch them every night.

4. I get a _____ from going on haunted hayrides with my friends.

5. My little brother is very _____ to loud noises and should not go to a haunted house.

C. Choose three words from the box in Part B. Use each word in a sentence.

1. _____

   _____

2. _____

   _____

3. _____

   _____

"That Was Scary! Let's Do It Again!"

Collaborative Discussion Support

Reread the article "That Was Scary! Let's Do It Again!" on pp. 56–58 of the Student Book.
Complete the organizer below to prepare for the discussion on Student Book page 59.

Cite text evidence to support your ideas.

Why does being scared make us feel good?	Text evidence
_____ _____ _____ _____	_____ _____ _____ _____
Does being scared always make us feel good?	**Text evidence**
_____ _____ _____ _____	_____ _____ _____ _____
Why do our bodies release chemicals when we are scared?	**Text evidence**
_____ _____ _____ _____	_____ _____ _____ _____
What is the main idea of this article?	**Text evidence**
We like to be scared when _____ _____ *because* _____ _____	_____ _____ _____ _____

Use with the Collaborative Discussion on **Student Book** page 59.

Figurative Language

A. For each item, choose the hyperbole. Circle it.

1. a. The chef made enough food to feed an army.

   b. The chef cooked six whole turkeys.

2. a. Her purse is filled with books!

   b. Her purse weighs a ton.

3. a. I told you once this morning and again this afternoon to take out the garbage.

   b. I've told you a million times to take the trash out.

B. Rewrite each sentence in your own words.

1. When I heard that there might be a blizzard I was scared to death.

_____

_____

_____

2. I sped down the sidewalk on my bike, fast as lightning!

_____

_____

_____

3. I have a ton of homework to do tonight.

_____

_____

_____

C. Use each of the hyperboles from Part B in a new sentence.

1. _____

_____

2. _____

_____

3. _____

_____

Context Clues

A. Circle the correct answer beneath each question with an underlined word. If necessary, use context clues and the dictionary to help you choose the correct answer.

1. Which is an example of an <u>exhilarating</u> experience?

   a. winning first prize in the science contest   **b.** falling asleep at the beach

2. If you <u>encounter</u> a wild animal in a dark alley, how will you probably feel?

   a. afraid   **b.** sleepy

3. If you are <u>sensitive</u> to criticism, how are you likely to feel when someone criticizes you?

   a. relieved   **b.** upset

4. If a building is <u>collapsing</u>, what is happening?

   a. The building is falling down.   **b.** The building is being rebuilt.

5. If you escape from a dangerous situation <u>unscathed</u>, what has happened to you?

   a. you are mildly, but not seriously, injured   **b.** nothing; you are unharmed

exhilarating	encounter	sensitive	collapsing
unscathed	genuine	coursing	ensures

B. Complete each sentence with the correct word from the box.

1. If your campaign for class president is _____, it is falling apart.

2. If your interest in saving endangered species like the tiger is _____, you will back up your words with action.

3. If you _____ someone you like but haven't seen for a long time, you will probably feel happy.

4. Studying hard _____ that you will improve your grades.

5. If you want an _____ experience, try riding a roller coaster.

C. Choose four words from the box. Use each word in a sentence.

1. _____

2. _____

3. _____

4. _____

Gerunds as Direct Objects and Objects of Prepositions

A. Decide which word in the sentence is the gerund. Circle the correct answer.

1. You really disappointed me by saying that.

    a. really   **b.** that   **c.** saying   **d.** disappointed

2. Ned isn't interested in learning to skate.

    a. interested   **b.** learning   **c.** skate   **d.** isn't

3. I'm a big fan of roasting vegetables.

    a. roasting   **b.** I'm   **c.** big   **d.** vegetables

4. This store stopped selling chocolate bars last year.

    a. last   **b.** stopped   **c.** This   **d.** selling

B. Fill in each blank with a gerund.

1. We've got plans for _____ this project on time.

2. You can learn about _____ with me!

3. I'm not going to stop _____ this sweater until it's done.

4. The whole class is sick of _____ for the test.

5. Shay went for a run because she loves _____ her heart rate up.

C. Choose one topic and write four sentences about it. Include at least one gerund as a direct object and at least one gerund as the object of a preposition in your paragraph. Possible topics:

compare yourself now to yourself as a little kid	make up a monster and describe it	what would you ban if you were the ruler of the world?

1. _____

_____

2. _____

_____

3. _____

_____

4. _____

_____

Sensory Details

As you listen to the podcast, map the story using the 5 W's: Who? What? Where? When? and Why? Pay attention to the sensory details and events as the plot develops. You may use the chart on page 61.

Who are the main characters in this story?

What is the narrator's conflict?

_____

_____

Details_____

_____

Where did the majority of the story take place?

Details_____

_____

_____

When did the act occur?

Supporting Details _____

_____

_____

Why did he confess?

_____

_____

_____

Supporting Details _____

_____

_____

Collaborative Discussion Support

Underline the key word or words in the Word Choice column. Determine the tone of the words and phrases from "The Tell-Tale Heart:" positive, negative or neutral. Then identify the emotion or mood the words create.

Word Choice	Tone +, −, neutral	Mood Created: How does it make you feel?
the old man sprang up in bed, crying out		
For a whole hour I did not move a muscle		
It increased my fury, as the beating of a drum stimulates the soldier into courage.		
And now a new anxiety seized me—the sound would be heard by a neighbor!		
I then smiled gaily, to find the deed so far done.		

What is the overall tone of the story?

_____

_____

_____

What mood or atmosphere does that create for the reader?

_____

_____

_____

How does the author maintain the mood?

_____

_____

_____

Academic Vocabulary

A. Complete each sentence with the correct word from the box.

predict	prediction	predictable	unpredictable

1. It was not _____ that the rookie singer would win the music prize.

2. If you use text clues, you may be able to _____ what will happen in a story.

3. Scientists consider different factors before making a _____ about population growth or climate change.

4. Sophia packed an umbrella just in case because the weather has been so _____ this week.

B. Complete each sentence.

1. I can predict what we will have for supper when _____
_____.

2. I don't think that a computer can predict _____
_____.

3. I think that _____ are unpredictable.

C. Using a word from the box, write a sentence about a prediction that you made that turned out to be true.

_____

_____

_____

_____

_____

_____

_____

_____

_____

_____

Critical Vocabulary

A. Read the sentences below. Circle the definition of each underlined word. Remember that you can look up any unfamiliar words in the dictionary.

1. I <u>trembled</u> after reading such a creepy story. *Trembled* means

   a. shook.   **b.** laughed.   **c.** cried.

2. My brother <u>wadded</u> up my favorite comic into a ball and threw it in the trash. *Wadded* means

   a. ripped.   **b.** organized.   **c.** crumpled.

3. I <u>stacked</u> all my books on the shelf. *Stacked* means

   a. arranged in an orderly pile.   **b.** jumbled in a heap.   **c.** attached.

4. My friend pranked me by lying <u>lifeless</u> on the couch. *Lifeless* means

   a. alone.   **b.** sprawled out.   **c.** motionless.

B. Choose a word from the box to complete each sentence. Write the word.

lifeless	stacked	tottering	howled
babbling	wadded	trembled	

1. My _____ baby sister makes strange noises.

2. The dog _____ at the moon.

3. The man was _____ down the staircase in the dark.

4. I _____ in fear when the lights went out.

C. Choose three words from the box in Part B. Use each word in a sentence.

1. _____

   _____

2. _____

   _____

3. _____

   _____

Compound Words

Remember, some compound words are written as one word, some are written as two words, and some are written with a hyphen.

living room	someplace	fire engine	baby steps	windshield
something	baby talk	breakfast	wrapping paper	

A. Choose a word from the box to answer each question.

1. Which word means "speech used by very young children"? _____

2. Which word means "the first meal of the day"? _____

3. Which word means "the front window of an aircraft, bus, car, or train"? _____

4. Which word means "decorative paper for presents"? _____

B. Complete each sentence with a compound word from the box.

1. The _____ raced down the street headed to the house on fire.

2. We set the Christmas tree up in the _____.

3. It's been a long winter, and Chad just wants to go to _____ warm.

4. The car's _____ was cracked and had to be fixed.

5. Adam took unsteady _____ across the kitchen floor.

C. Choose four words from the box. Use each word in a sentence.

1. _____

   _____

2. _____

   _____

3. _____

   _____

4. _____

   _____

Collaborative Discussion Support

Use the questions below to evaluate the use of dialogue in "Little Brother™."

1. How is dialogue used to set the tone on page 63?

_____

_____

_____

_____

2. How is dialogue used to set the scene on page 63?

_____

_____

_____

_____

3. How is dialogue used to show a shift in the characters' feelings on page 64?

_____

_____

_____

_____

4. How are the mother's feelings about Little Brother™ revealed on page 65?

_____

_____

_____

_____

5. Peter's responses to his mother on pages 63 and 65 are exactly the same. What does this reveal about Peter's relationship with his mother?

_____

_____

_____

6. What does the conflict on page 66 reveal about each character?

_____

_____

_____

_____

Response to Literature

Answer the questions to help you prepare a short response to "Little Brother™."

1. What was your reaction to the surprise ending?

_____

_____

_____

_____

_____

2. Why was the ending surprising?

_____

_____

_____

_____

_____

3. How does the ending connect this story to the theme of the unit, "The Thrill of Horror"?

_____

_____

_____

_____

_____

4. Use your responses above to write a short response to "Little Brother™."

_____

_____

_____

_____

_____

Denotation and Connotation

| cockroach | hen | hornet | mule | pig | rat | sheep |

A. Choose the word from the box that best completes each sentence.

1. Jake is a sneaky _____ and cannot be trusted.

2. When Marla makes up her mind you cannot change it because she is as stubborn as a
_____

3. You better have plenty of food if you ask Fred to dinner because he eats like a _____ .

4. Bill is like a _____; no matter how many times you kick him out, he keeps on showing up again.

5. The whole group of them are like _____; whatever Carl tells them to do they do without even thinking.

| smell | speak | take | big | curious |

B. Write a synonym for each of the words in the box. Choose a synonym with a negative connotation.

1. _____
2. _____
3. _____
4. _____
5. _____

| baboon | bull | hog | hornet | horse |

C. Choose four words from the box. Use each word to describe a person in a sentence. Each sentence should show that you understand the connotative meaning of the word as you have used it.

1. _____
2. _____
3. _____
4. _____

Infinitives as Subjects and Subject Complements

A. Decide whether the infinitive in the sentence is the subject or the subject complement. Circle the correct answer.

1. To help people is admirable.   (subject, subject complement)

2. All I want is to go home.   (subject, subject complement)

3. To eat pomegranates takes some effort.   (subject, subject complement)

4. The best feeling in the world is to fall in love.   (subject, subject complement)

B. Fill in the blanks with an infinitive.

1. _____ your room can be a pain, but it's worth it.

2. _____ a car takes a lot of expertise.

3. It's easy _____; all you have to do is move to the beat.

4. I wish it were that simple _____.

5. The goal with this project is _____ gravity.

C. Choose one topic and write four sentences on that topic. Include at least one infinitive as a subject and at least one infinitive as a subject complement in your paragraph. Possible topics:

describe something you do regularly that you think more people should try	describe a habit you'd like to break	describe dinner in your household

1. _____

_____

2. _____

_____

3. _____

_____

4. _____

_____

Critical Vocabulary

A. Read the sentences below. Circle the definition of each underlined word. Remember that you can look up any unfamiliar words in the dictionary.

1. The room filled with <u>gloom</u> when we heard our team had lost.

   a. sadness.   **b.** glee.   **c.** confusion.

2. The fly began its <u>idiotic</u> dance beside John's bed. *Idiotic* means

   a. funny.   **b.** loud.   **c.** foolish.

3. So boredom led to anger and then anger led to <u>spite</u>. *Spite* means

   a. boredom.   **b.** relief.   **c.** malice.

4. A <u>monstrous</u> hand crushed the fly. *Monstrous* means

   a. very large.   **b.** petite.   **c.** bony.

B. Choose a word from the box to complete each sentence.

spite	gloom	struggling	idiotic	ambled	corpse	monstrous

1. The fly's _____ was crushed.

2. I could see the fly _____ in John's hand.

3. John's mother _____ slowly into the room.

4. To _____ the fly, I wanted to finally trap it.

C. Choose three words from the box in Part B. Use each word in a sentence.

1. _____

   _____

   _____

2. _____

   _____

   _____

3. _____

   _____

   _____

Build Vocabulary

Academic Vocabulary

A. Complete each sentence with the correct word from the box.

psychological	psychologist	psychology

1. Ursula writes stories that have a lot of _____ complexity.

2. Richard's _____ is that everything will turn out fine if he thinks positive thoughts.

3. Zoey majored in _____ when she was in college.

4. Dr. Nossiter studies the _____ of persuasion, which means he studies why people say "yes."

B. Complete each sentence.

1. If I were a psychologist, I would study _____

_____.

2. I feel psychological benefits when _____

_____.

C. Using one of the words in the box, write a sentence about how studying psychology can help others.

psychological	psychologist	psychology

_____

_____

_____

_____

_____

_____

_____

_____

_____

_____

Collaborative Discussion Support

Use the prompts below to gather your thoughts about poetic form in "John Sebastian Huntingdon."

So John Sebastian Huntingdon ___ ___
sat upstairs in his room. ___ ___
The day had gone on far too long ___ ___
and nothing much was going on — ___ ___
a fly had been the only thing ___ ___
to penetrate the gloom. ___ ___
All afternoon. ___ ___

So boredom led to anger ___ ___
and then anger led to spite ___ ___
(and spite is really frightening). ___ ___
John's hand was fast as lightning — ___ ___
it closed around the insect so ___ ___
the fly was not in flight. ___ ___
But still all right. ___ ___

A boy does have some power, though ___ ___
To help him with a plan. ___ ___
John stopped the fly from struggling ___ ___
and started pulling off one wing, ___ ___
surprised at just how easily ___ ___
it came off in his hand. ___ ___
He's superman! ___ ___

And then John's mother ambled in ___ ___
And startled superman. ___ ___
With some alarm she saw the harm ___ ___
And grabbed that bully by the arm, ___ ___
surprised at just how easily ___ ___
it came off in her hand. ___ ___
Her monstrous hand. ___ ___

Looking at Form

1. How many lines are in each stanza? _____

2. Count the syllables in each line. Label each line with the number of syllables it contains. Recite the poem aloud to yourself. Listen for the syllables in the words. Do they create a pattern? What is another word for *pattern* that applies to the poem? You may use a dictionary to find synonyms for *pattern*.

_____
_____
_____

3. Go through the poem and letter the rhyming lines in each stanza using the letters A, B, C, D. What rhyme pattern do you notice?

_____
_____
_____
_____

4. Reread the last stanza. What effect does the repetition of the word "hand" have?

_____
_____
_____
_____

Multiple-Meaning Words

A. Choose the response that correctly defines the underlined word as it is used in the sentence.

1. The head chef decides on the restaurant's menu.

   a. the one in charge   **b.** to lead something or a group of people

2. Jorge injured his hand playing basketball.

   a. body part of the end of the arm   **b.** cards held by players in a card game

3. I love to dance especially to salsa music.

   a. a formal performance set to music   **b.** to move one's body in rhythm to music

4. Fransisco has a natural head for math.

   a. aptitude or talent   **b.** the upper part of an animal that includes the brain

B. Define each underlined word as it is used in each sentence.

1. I looked at my cards and realized I had a great hand.

   _____

2. Because the flight was delayed for three hours, most of the passengers were cranky.

   _____

3. Roberto will hand in his report in on Tuesday.

   _____

4. One little, buzzing fly annoyed almost everyone at the picnic.

   _____

fly	dance	head	wing	hand

C. Choose a word from the box. Use each word in two sentences that show different meanings of the word.

1. Word: _____

   Sentence: _____

   _____

   Sentence: _____

   _____

Performance Task

Writing Activity: Twist Ending

Work with a partner or on your own to write a short story that has a twist ending. Answer the questions below to help you plan your story.

1. What is the setting? _____
_____
_____
_____

2. Who are the characters? _____
_____
_____
_____

3. What are the events that make up the rising action? _____
_____
_____
_____
_____

4. What is the climax? _____
_____
_____
_____
_____

5. What is the resolution? _____
_____
_____
_____
_____

6. What is the falling action? _____
_____
_____
_____
_____

Build Vocabulary

Homophones

A. Circle the correct homophone.

1. Which word means "to put words on paper"?

   a. right   **b.** write

2. Which word means "the number 4"?

   a. for   **b.** four

3. Which word means "it is"?

   a. it's   **b.** its

4. Which word means "was successful"?

   a. won   **b.** one

5. Which word means "to cry very loudly"?

   a. bawl   **b.** ball

B. Complete each sentence with the correct homophone.

1. Jose spent hours playing _____ with the dog. (ball, bawl)

2. Maria is going _____ a walk after lunch. (for, four)

3. _____ your name and address in the blank. (right, write)

4. Phillipe got every answer _____. (right, write)

5. Kim is the _____ who received first prize. (one, won)

to/too/two	for/four	one/won	right/write	its/it's	ball/bawl

C. Choose three homophone sets from the box. Use each word in a sentence.

1. homophones: _____ and _____

   _____

   _____

2. homophones: _____ and _____

   _____

   _____

3. homophones: _____ and _____

   _____

   _____

Specialized Vocabulary

optimist	pessimistic	supernatural	realism
journalist	horror	absurdity	style

A. Choose the correct word from the box to answer each question. You can use a dictionary to help you if needed.

1. What word describes the particular way a writer writes? _____

2. What is something that causes strong feelings of fear, dread, or shock? _____

3. What word describes someone who always expects the worst to happen? _____

4. What word means something that is silly, foolish, or unreasonable? _____

5. What word describes someone who writes or edits stories or news reports? _____

B. Complete each sentence with the correct word from the box.

1. As a _____, Marcia travelled all over the word to cover the news.

2. David was an incurable _____, always hopeful about the future.

3. Michelle is fascinated by the _____ and likes watching movies about ghosts.

4. Greta felt such a profound sense of _____ that she could hardly speak.

5. The _____ of thinking they would actually win the game now that they were twenty points behind made Kevin laugh right out loud.

C. Choose five words from the box. Use each word in a sentence.

1. _____

_____

2. _____

_____

3. _____

_____

4. _____

_____

5. _____

_____

Infinitives as Direct Objects and Objects of Prepositions

A. Decide whether the infinitive in the sentence is a direct object or the object of a preposition. Circle the correct answer.

1. Eric wants to send Kay a message.   (direct object   object of preposition)

2. I've been trying to watch this show all day.   (direct object   object of preposition)

3. There are no options left except to wait.   (direct object   object of preposition)

4. If you want information, you have no choice but to ask for it.   (direct object   object of preposition)

B. Fill in the blanks with an infinitive.

1. Do you like _____ romance novels?

2. Nothing was left to do save _____ the package.

3. Would you prefer _____ over the phone?

4. I don't need anything except _____ healthy and safe.

5. Candy hoped _____ a new book.

C. Choose one topic and write four sentences about it. Include at least one infinitive as a direct object and at least one infinitive as the object of a preposition in your paragraph. Possible topics:

Describe an object in the room in detail	Write about moving house	Describe a chore you don't like

1. _____

   _____

2. _____

   _____

3. _____

   _____

4. _____

   _____

The Influence of Experiences

Review the selection on Student Book pages 72–75. How might Ambrose Bierce's experiences have influenced his writing? What forces might have been responsible for building (or changing) his character? What do you know about Bierce's writing? Cite examples from the text.

Bierce's Experiences

_____
_____
_____
_____
_____
_____
_____
_____
_____
_____
_____
_____
_____
_____
_____
_____
_____
_____
_____
_____
_____
_____

Bierce's Character

_____
_____
_____
_____
_____
_____
_____
_____
_____
_____
_____

Bierce's Writing

_____
_____
_____
_____
_____
_____
_____
_____
_____

Academic Vocabulary

A. Complete each sentence.

1. If I had to write a movie summary, I would write about _____ because
   _____
   _____
   _____

2. I can summarize today's lesson by saying that we _____
   _____
   _____
   _____

B. Read the passage and answer the questions.

> Annie wants to become a film critic because she has a lot to say about the movies she
> sees. After she watches a movie, she practices summarizing the plot and describing
> the main characters. Since it is important for a critic to write his or her own reactions
> to the movie, she writes about what she thinks and feels. The last paragraph is usually
> a summary of the main things she liked and didn't like about the film.

1. What does Annie practice summarizing?

   She practices _____ .

2. What should the last paragraph be?

   It usually should be a _____
   _____ .

summary	summarize

C. Using a form of one of the words from the box, write a brief summary of what you
did yesterday.

_____
_____
_____
_____

Critical Vocabulary

A. Read the sentences below. Circle the definition of each underlined word. Remember that you can look up any unfamiliar words in the dictionary.

1. Searching for the secret of life became Dr. Frankenstein's true passion. *Passion* means

    a. desire.   **b.** dislike.   **c.** objection.

2. I would pursue my creation to the ends of the earth. *Pursue* means

    a. ignore.   **b.** follow.   **c.** love.

3. Overcome with grief and guilt, I looked for refuge in the mountains. A *refuge* is

    a. a shelter.   **b.** a civilization.   **c.** a new life.

4. Dr. Frankenstein reluctantly made his monster a bride. *Reluctantly* means

    a. wholeheartedly.   **b.** unwillingly.   **c.** enthusiastically.

B. Choose a word from the box to complete each sentence.

passion	horrified	unburden	refuge
misery	reluctantly	pursue	devoted

1. Dr. Frankenstein was _____ to making his new creation.

2. He had so much on his mind, he needed to _____ himself of his troubles.

3. Dr. Frankenstein wanted to _____ his scientific goals and interests.

4. The man was _____ as he listened to the scary tale.

5. The story of Frankenstein's monster is a sad tale of _____.

C. Choose three words from the box in Part B. Use each word in a sentence.

1. _____

    _____

2. _____

    _____

3. _____

    _____

The Prefixes *mis*– and *re*–

misfortunes	misinform	returns	reconsider
miscount	misread	retell	recreate

A. Choose a word from the box to answer each question. Remember you can use the dictionary to help you if needed.

1. What word means "to read something incorrectly"? _____

2. What word means "to think about something again"? _____

3. What word means "bad luck"? _____

4. What word means "to give incorrect information"? _____

5. What word means "comes back"? _____

B. Complete each sentence with a word from the box.

1. Even though we've heard the story before, we constantly ask my father to _____ it.

2. The painting was ruined, and Tamika didn't know if she could _____ it.

3. Would you please _____ my offer to fix your bike?

4. My family _____ to the camp site every summer.

5. Be careful and concentrate, otherwise you may _____ the number of items in the box.

C. Choose three words from the box. Use each word in a sentence.

1. _____

   _____

   _____

2. _____

   _____

   _____

3. _____

   _____

   _____

Collaborative Discussion Support

Look through *Frankenstein* on Student Book pages 77–83. Find information to answer the questions below.

Why does Frankenstein make the creature?

_____

_____

_____

_____

How does he feel about the success of his work?

_____

_____

_____

_____

How does the creature feel about his life?

_____

_____

_____

_____

What events result from Frankenstein's work?

_____

_____

_____

_____

Use your answers for the Collaborative Discussion on **Student Book** page 84.

Short Response

Make notes below to help you complete the Performance Task on Student Book page 84.
Note evidence from the selection that you can cite when you write.

What is the theme of "Frankenstein"?

Text evidence

How did Frankenstein feel about his work before he created the creature?

Text evidence

How did he feel after he created the creature? What contributed to his feelings?

Text evidence

What does the text directly say about the feelings of the creature?

Text evidence

What can you infer about the feelings of the creature?

Text evidence

How do the events of the text support your understanding of the theme?

Text evidence

USE WITH STUDENT BOOK pp. 76–83

Visual Clues

glimpse	horrified	unburden	refuge

A. Choose the best answer to complete each sentence.

1. We tried to _____ the young man of his problems and worries.

a. glimpse   **b.** unburden

2. I caught a _____ of the thief as he rounded the corner trying to outrun the police.

a. refuge   **b.** glimpse

3. Marlena was _____ to learn that her dog had escaped and was nowhere to be found.

a. refuge   **b.** horrified

4. Olivia's _____, the place where she goes when she's upset, is the river bank not far from her home.

a. refuge   **b.** glimpse

B. Choose the word from the box that most closely fits each of the following descriptions of an illustration.

1. an ugly, disfigured creature; in the backgroud, Frankenstein turning his back and leaving the room

_____

2. Frankenstein looking out the window to see a person in the shadows running

_____

3. a very upset Dr. Frankenstein, hiding in the mountains

_____

C. Choose two words from the box. Use each word in a sentence that is <u>not</u> about Frankenstein, the creature, or the story's narrator. Write the sentences in the space.

1. _____

_____

2. _____

_____

Infinitives: Special Case

A. **Decide whether the infinitive in the sentence is a direct object or a special case. Circle the correct answer.**

1. Mati advised me to watch my cat carefully.   (direct object   special case)

2. They decided to go to the movies.   (direct object   special case)

3. Let's plan to start making dinner at six.   (direct object   special case)

4. The recipe instructs us to measure three cups of water.   (direct object   special case)

B. **Fill in the blanks with an infinitive.**

1. I told my cat _____ down, but she didn't listen.

2. The rules permit anyone _____ as long as they have registered for the contest.

3. Mama reminded me _____ eggs on my way home from school.

4. I invite you _____ yourself comfortable.

5. You can't force someone _____ with you.

C. **Choose one topic and write four sentences about it. Include at least two special case infinitives in your paragraph. Possible topics:**

Advice for how to take care of yourself when you're sick	Explain to someone else how to make a sandwich (or some other simple food)	Advice you would give to a new student at your school

1. _____

   _____

2. _____

   _____

3. _____

   _____

4. _____

   _____

Model a Soliloquy

Read the Speak Out! assignment on p. 85 of the Student Book. Answer the questions below to help you create the soliloquy you will perform.

What question do you think the creature would ask Victor Frankenstein?

_____

_____

_____

_____

_____

How would the creature describe his life?

_____

_____

_____

_____

_____

What would the creature say about the way people treat him?

_____

_____

_____

_____

_____

What is the last thing the creature would say to Frankenstein?

_____

_____

_____

_____

_____

Build Vocabulary

Word Families

university	confide	creature	executed

A. Choose a word from the box to answer each question.

1. Which word means "to carry out"? _____

2. Which word means "to tell someone something private or secret"? _____

3. Which word means "an institution of higher learning"? _____

4. Which word means "an animal of any kind"? _____

B. Complete the sentences with the correct word from the box.

1. The state will _____ the prisoner on June 5th.

2. I trust my best friend and often _____ my secrets to her.

3. As an animal lover, Jay believes we should be kind to every living _____.

4. My sister cannot decide which _____ she wants to attend.

C. Write four sentences. In each sentence use one word from the box.

1. _____

   _____

   _____

2. _____

   _____

   _____

3. _____

   _____

   _____

4. _____

   _____

   _____

Short Story Ideas

You will be writing a short story about the thrill of horror. The first step is writing down your story ideas.

A. Circle the items in each box that you find interesting or exciting.

Realistic	Imaginary
• the first day of school	• a day spent lost in a deserted city
• an experience during a blackout	• an experience during an invasion from another world
• a meeting with a stranger who knows your name	• a meeting with a being who is not human
• a visit to a cemetery on a foggy day	• finding a cemetery in your backyard
• getting trapped in the basement	• getting trapped in another dimension
• exploring a cave full of bats	• exploring a hole to a different time

Give yourself story ideas. Fill in the blanks and provide two examples of other situations that you find horrific, frightening, or exciting.

I think _____ is frightening.

I think _____ is horrific.

_____

_____

B. Write three ideas about situations for your short story. Remember, you can use a real experience, a fictional one, or a combination.

Idea 1 _____

_____

_____

Idea 2 _____

_____

_____

Idea 3 _____

_____

_____

Plan Your Story

To evaluate your work, use the Short Story Rubric available from your online Student Resources or from your teacher.

Conflict

What is the problem or struggle that your characters face?

_____

_____

Characters

The main character is _____

Other characters are _____

Describe what your main character looks like.

_____

Describe your main character's personality.

_____

Setting

Describe the place.

_____

Describe the time (daytime, nighttime, season, past, present, future).

_____

Point of View

First person: I, We
Third person: He, She, They

Which point of view will you use?

_____

_____

_____

_____

Academic Vocabulary

A. Complete each sentence with the correct word from the box.

| technical | techniques | technically |

1. Detectives learn a lot of _____ to find clues and solve crimes.

2. When Adam plays the violin, every note is _____ right.

3. When the engineer spoke, her language was too _____ for me to understand.

4. The race finished with a tie because we couldn't tell who _____ came in first.

B. Read the passage and answer the questions.

Enrique's dad was a cook in the navy, where he learned great techniques for feeding large groups. This comes in handy at Thanksgiving. He sets up a tamale-making assembly line, and the tamales come out technically perfect. But all of his technical ability is necessary to get all of the food ready at the same time.

1. What did Enrique's dad learn in the navy?

   He learned techniques for _____

2. How do his tamales come out?

   The tamales _____

3. What kind of ability is necessary to get all the food exactly on time?

   _____ ability is necessary.

| technique | technical | technically |

C. Using a word from the box, write a sentence about a technique you have learned and what you do with it.

_____

_____

_____

_____

_____

_____

_____

Finalize Your Plan

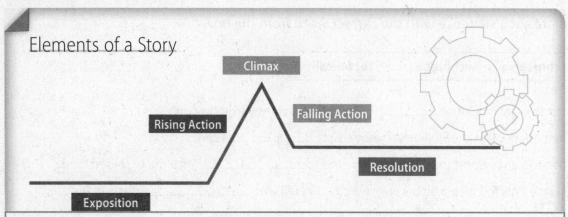

Elements of a Story

Climax

Rising Action

Falling Action

Resolution

Exposition

Exposition – Introduce your main character, setting, and conflict.

Rising Action – Introduce the obstacles the character must overcome. Build suspense.

Climax – The most important or exciting section of the story.

Falling Action – How the conflict is resolved and the lesson the character learns.

Resolution – The final part of the plot.

A. Review the elements of a story above. Describe the elements that you will include in your short story.

Exposition _____

_____

Rising Action _____

_____

Climax _____

_____

Falling Action _____

_____

Resolution _____

_____

B. Write a brief summary of your story.

_____

_____

_____

Vocabulary Review

Here are some of the words you learned in this unit. Choose words from this list and sort them into the categories below. There are many possible correct answers! Many of the words fit into more than one category.

absurdity	dread	menacing	recreate	technical
alert	encounter	miscount	refuge	terror
anxiety	ensures	misfortunes	retell	thumping
babbling	fear	misinform	returns	tottering
baby steps	fire engine	misread	scratching	trembled
basketball	flight	optimist	screeching	trepidation
bawl	fright	panic	self-esteem	unburden
breakfast	genuine	post office	sensitive	university
collapsing	hissing	predict	someplace	unscathed
conventional	hornet	psychological	something	wadded
coursing	howled	rattling	spooky	whispering
disquiet	lifeless	realism	stacked	windshield
distracted	living room	reconsider	summarize	wrapping paper

Compound Words

1. _____
2. _____
3. _____
4. _____
5. _____

Words that Signify Sounds

1. _____
2. _____
3. _____
4. _____
5. _____

Words with Prefixes

1. _____
2. _____
3. _____
4. _____
5. _____

Synonyms for "Horror"

1. _____
2. _____
3. _____
4. _____
5. _____

Easily Confused Words

A. Decide which word makes sense. Circle the correct answer.

1. (Proceed   Precede)   calmly out of the building in the case of a fire.

2. Every   (our   hour)   the clock strikes.

3. For some reason, the primary source I want is   (alluding   eluding)   me.

4. These tracks   (imply   infer)   that someone has been here recently.

B. Fill in the blanks with a word that fits.

1. This manuscript is so old, it _____ the printing press.

2. The poem I read _____ to, but didn't mention, earlier works by the same author.

3. Caffe Bene is _____ favorite coffee shop.

4. A careful scholar can _____ a lot beyond what a text explicitly states.

5. The bandit _____ capture for almost fifteen years.

C. Choose one topic and write four sentences about it. Use at least one word from each pair of easily confused words in your paragraph (*proceed/precede, hour/our, imply/infer, allude/elude*). Make sure that the context of each sentence demonstrates that you understand the meaning of the word. Possible topics:

A spooky experience that happened to you	Trick-or-treating	Getting ready to go out with friends

1. _____
   _____

2. _____
   _____

3. _____
   _____

4. _____
   _____

The Move Toward Freedom

"Those who deny freedom to others deserve it not for themselves."

—Abraham Lincoln, U.S. President

What do you think of when you hear the word "freedom"? You can make visual notes or write.

What animal do you think of when you think of freedom?

_____

_____

What activity do you connect with freedom?

_____

_____

Name two freedoms that are really important to you.

_____

_____

What is one freedom that people don't have until they are adults?

_____

_____

What could you do to increase the freedom of others?

_____

_____

Academic Vocabulary

As you work through Unit 3, look and listen for these words. Practice using them when you talk in class and in your writing. Write about your experiences using these words in the last column of the chart.

Word	Definition	Related Forms	My Experiences
access	• the right or ability to enter, look at, or use something • to enter, look at, or use something	accessible, accessibility	
civil	related to citizens	civilization, civilian, civil rights	
demonstrate	• to show or prove something clearly and carefully	demonstration, demonstrable	
document	• a written or printed paper • to provide evidence for	documentary, documentation	
symbolize	to be a symbol of, or represent something	symbol, symbolic, symbolism	

Personalized Similes

Use the chart to makes notes for creating a simile that completes the phrase *as free as* with a person's name. Choose two people and explore how each is free.

Simile about a person as free as:	
Explain why this person suggests freedom to you.	_____ _____ _____ _____ _____ _____ _____ _____ _____ _____

Simile about a person as free as:	
Explain why this person suggests freedom to you.	_____ _____ _____ _____ _____ _____ _____ _____ _____ _____

Creating Similes

Write a story about a family experience that you remember clearly. Think of similes that describe the actions and characters (family members, pets). Remember to use the words *like* or *as* when you make your comparisons. Be sure to use at least three similes in your story.

_____

_____

_____

_____

_____

_____

_____

_____

_____

_____

_____

_____

_____

_____

_____

_____

_____

_____

_____

_____

_____

_____

_____

_____

_____

Collaborative Discussion

Make notes for the Collaborative Discussion on "Every Blog Has Its Day." Read the prompt on page 96 of the Student Book to complete this page.

Discussing the Purpose

What is the central idea of the blog post?

_____

_____

_____

_____

What points does the writer make?

_____

_____

_____

_____

Evidence from the text:

_____

_____

_____

_____

Language Choices

How has the blogger used language to support the points and present them reasonably? Cite evidence.

_____

_____

_____

softening statements

_____

_____

_____

Critical Vocabulary

A. Read the sentences below. Circle the definition of each underlined word. Remember that you can look up any unfamiliar words in the dictionary.

1. Freedom can mean freedom from injustice.

   a. correctness   **b.** politics   **c.** unfairness

2. We live in a society where rules protect our property.

   a. food we grow   **b.** things we own   **c.** big companies

3. I hope nothing interferes with my getting to Matt's house in time to help him with his project.

   a. does business   **b.** gets in the way   **c.** agrees

4. I have a good excuse for not finishing my reading assignment; the storm blew out the electrical lights last night!

   a. reason   **b.** behavior   **c.** offense

B. Choose a word from the box to complete each sentence.

injustice	property	interferes	afford	obedience	excuse

1. The newspaper reporter thinks it is his job to inform people about _____ so they can do something about it.

2. I forgot my wallet at home, so I can't _____ to buy a newspaper today!

3. Tyrants expect complete _____ from all of the citizens in the country.

4. I don't think he likes soccer because every time we invite him to a game he gives a different _____.

C. Choose two words from the box in Part B. Use each word in a sentence.

1. _____
   _____
   _____

2. _____
   _____
   _____

Writing a Blog

To evaluate your blog, use the Blog Rubric available from your online Student Resources or from your teacher.

Choose a Topic

Use these questions to help you choose a design for your blog.

1. What words would I use to describe the look I would like to have? Circle two or three.
   Add your own words in the blank.

   - beautiful
   - fun
   - creative
   - cheerful

   - edgy
   - clean
   - dark
   - flashy

   - different
   - bold
   - _____
   - _____

2. What colors would give me the look I want? Circle as many as you like.

   - bright red
   - dark red
   - yellow
   - orange
   - light brown
   - dark brown

   - dark blue
   - light blue
   - bright blue
   - lavender
   - purple
   - pink

   - dark green
   - bright green
   - pale green
   - black
   - _____
   - _____

3. What features would I like? Circle as many as you like.
   (The more you choose, the more work you'll have to do!)

   - favorite links
   - blog archive

   - photo gallery
   - registration

   - _____
   - _____

Synonyms

A. Replace the words in parentheses with a synonym from the box.

| fretting | conformity | thieves | rules | limits | extravagant | suddenly |

1. If my family ever won the lottery, we would probably take (fancy) _____ vacations several times a year.

2. While our neighbors were away on vacation, (bandits) _____ broke into their home and stole their computer.

3. We were driving along the road when my aunt (abruptly) _____ slammed on the brakes to avoid colliding with a large deer.

4. Even though I knew my dad was an excellent driver, I couldn't help (worrying) _____ about him being out in the snowstorm.

5. The (regulations) _____ for the community pool seem overly strict, but I know they were developed to keep everyone safe.

6. While freedom of speech is important, I believe there should be some (restrictions) _____ on what people are allowed to say.

B. Write two synonyms for each word. You can use a dictionary or thesaurus to help you.

1. conformity _____, _____

2. limits _____, _____

3. suddenly _____, _____

4. rules _____, _____

C. Choose two synonym pairs from Part B. Use each word in a sentence. Underline the synonyms.

Synonyms: _____ and _____

Sentence #1: _____

Sentence #2: _____

Synonyms: _____ and _____

Sentence #1: _____

Sentence #2: _____

Active and Passive Voice

A. Determine whether the sentence is active or passive. Circle the correct answer.

1. Millions of people watched the spectacular solar eclipse.   (active   passive)

2. Poems about freedom were written by the students.   (active   passive)

3. A team of experts tested the new seat belt.   (active   passive)

4. The orders for the new computers were checked more than five times.   (active   passive)

B. Rewrite each sentence to change the voice, making it active if it's passive, or passive if it's active.

1. Volunteers freed and cared for the abused dogs.

_____

2. We checked the glass for the telescope more than a hundred times.

_____

3. Some of the money was misplaced by Josh.

_____

4. The solitary child was noticed by only a few people.

_____

5. Simone and I answered all the questions.

_____

C. Choose one topic and write four sentences about it. Use at least two active sentences and at least two passive sentences. Possible topics:

the first day of summer vacation	playing a practical joke	an argument with a good friend

1. _____

2. _____

3. _____

4. _____

Sequence

Answer the questions about *Our Documentary*.

1. Who came first to the States in Alma's family?

_____

2. Who came first to the States in Dai's family?

_____

3. Who came first to the States in David's family?

_____

4. What happened next to Alma's family?

_____

_____

5. Describe Dai's experience after his arrival in America.

_____

_____

6. What happened to him afterwards?

_____

_____

7. How did David feel after arriving in San Diego?

_____

_____

Compare and Contrast

Think about the video you have just seen. Compare and contrast it with "Every Blog Has Its Day."

1. What common theme do the video and the blog share?

_____

_____

2. What similar experiences did the friends of the blogger and the people in the video go through?

_____

_____

3. How are the video and the blog different?

_____

_____

Critical Vocabulary

A. Circle four words in the Word Bank that you want to know more about.

Word Bank						
prepared	debate	trend	deduce	convince	performances	suffice
promote	negotiate	venue	destiny	responsibility	marketing	compliment

B. Watch the video *Nature At Work* again and listen for the words. Complete the activity.

1. Word: _____

What I think it means: _____

What it means: _____

2. Word: _____

What I think it means: _____

What it means: _____

3. Word: _____

What I think it means: _____

What it means: _____

4. Word: _____

What I think it means: _____

What it means: _____

C. Choose three words that you wrote in Part B. Write a sentence using each word.

1. _____

_____

2. _____

_____

3. _____

_____

Academic Vocabulary

A. Complete each sentence with the correct word from the box.

access	accessible	accessibility

1. The band released its songs free online because it wants its music to be _____ to more people.

2. If students had _____ to more resources, they could write better reports.

3. The _____ of air travel allows people to migrate more easily.

4. You can _____ the technical information under the Tools menu.

B. Complete each sentence.

1. If an island is not accessible by airplane, you can _____
   _____

2. If I did not have access to a school, I would _____
   _____

C. Write a paragraph about how you would adapt and modify a house to make it accessible to people in wheelchairs. Use all of the words in the box.

_____

_____

_____

_____

_____

_____

_____

_____

_____

_____

_____

Build Vocabulary

Critical Vocabulary

The vocabulary on this page was taken from "The Grand Mosque of Paris."

A. Read the sentences below. Circle the definition of each underlined word. Remember that you can look up any unfamiliar words in the dictionary.

1. Anyone who <u>encounters</u> one of his children must give that child shelter and protection for as long as misfortune—or sorrow—lasts.

   a. refers to   **b.** meets   **c.** needs

2. They were able to form a tight network and use Kabyle as a kind of <u>code</u>.

   a. iron pointer   **b.** safety net   **c.** secret language

3. The Resistance was a <u>clandestine</u> network of spies and fighters, made up of ordinary people who did whatever they could to fight the Nazis.

   a. iron pointer   **b.** safety net   **c.** secret

4. A story describes a deliveryman and his vehicle, a three-wheeled bicycle with a large <u>bin</u> attached to it.

   a. container   **b.** bell   **c.** chain

B. Choose a word from the box to complete each sentence.

encounters	clandestine	network	code	smuggle	bin

1. The Navajo language was also used as a _____ to transmit secret messages using military radios during World War II.

2. The Nazis could see by their hats that the Kabyles were Muslim, and they didn't think that Muslims were giving _____ help to the Jews.

3. The Kabyles worked together to _____ Jews out of Paris to safety.

4. The French Resistance was a loose _____ of individuals who worked secretly against the Nazis.

C. Choose three words from the box in Part B. Use each word in a sentence.

1. _____

2. _____

3. _____

Author's Purpose

Use the cluster diagram to prepare to discuss the authors' purpose for writing *The Grand Mosque of Paris*. In the center of the diagram is the authors' basic purpose—to inform the reader. Write what you think the authors' are telling the reader in each of the ovals. Ask yourself: What ideas and information are they conveying to the reader?

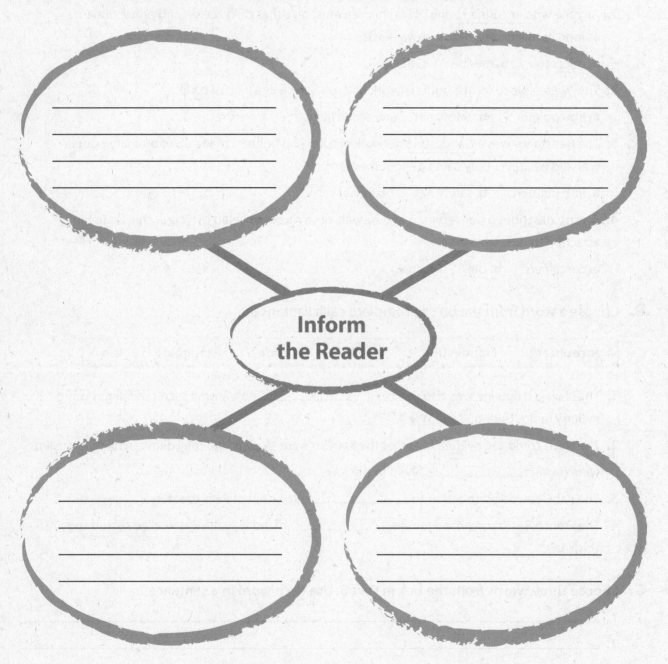

Inform the Reader

Sensory Adjectives

A. Read the sentences below. Each sentence has a sensory adjective underlined. Identify the sense each underlined adjective is appealing to. Write your answers on the lines.

1. I woke up in the middle of the night when it was still utterly <u>dark</u> outside my window. _____

2. The cat licked me with her <u>rough</u> tongue, which felt a little like sandpaper. _____

3. She pulled her hat down over her ears as she stepped out into the <u>chilly</u> winter air. _____

4. The <u>low</u> ceilings and the small size of the room made me feel like a mouse trapped inside a cage.

_____

B. Write two sensory adjectives for each of the five senses. Remember that sensory adjectives help a reader understand how something or someone looks, smells, feels, sounds, or tastes.

1. smell _____ , _____

2. sight _____ , _____

3. touch _____ , _____

4. taste _____ , _____

5. sound _____ , _____

C. Choose four sensory adjectives from Part B. Write four sentences using adjectives that appeal to four different senses. Underline the sensory adjectives and identify which sense each adjective is appealing to.

Sentence #1: _____

Sense adjective is appealing to: _____

Sentence #2: _____

Sense adjective is appealing to: _____

Sentence #3: _____

Sense adjective is appealing to: _____

Sentence #4: _____

Sense adjective is appealing to: _____

Latin Roots *Cent* and *Terr*

The Latin root *cent* means "one hundred." The Latin root *terr* means "earth."

A. Use the words in the box below to answer the questions.

subterranean	century	centimeter	percentage
centenarian	terrarium	terrestrial	terrain

1. Which word describes a proportion that is expressed in relation to one hundred parts?

   _____

2. Which word means "related to or of the earth"? _____

3. Which word refers to a period of one hundred years? _____

4. Which word describes a container that is used to house small land animals or plants?

   _____

5. Which word means "located beneath the earth's surface"? _____

6. Which word is used to refer to an area or tract of land? _____

B. Complete each sentence with a word from the box in Part A.

1. Anyone who hopes to one day be a _____ needs to eat a healthy diet and exercise regularly.

2. I used my ruler to verify that the insect was about one _____ long.

3. My truck is specially designed to go off road and drive smoothly over rough, uneven

   _____ .

4. I received a pet lizard and a large _____ to keep it in for my birthday.

5. A small _____ of the store's sales will be donated to the local homeless shelter.

C. Choose three words from the table in Part A. Use each word in a sentence. Underline the root *terr* or *cent* in each word.

1. _____

   _____

2. _____

   _____

3. _____

   _____

Active and Passive Voice

A. Determine whether the sentence is active or passive. Circle the correct answer.

1. Rachel was woken up by her alarm.   (active   passive)

2. I needed Willow to help me finish the project.   (active   passive)

3. At the grocery store, we found apples and oranges.   (active   passive)

4. My artistic skills were challenged by the assignment.   (active   passive)

B. Rewrite the sentence to change the voice, making it active if it was passive, or passive if it was active.

1. I'm fascinated by the history of my hometown. _____

   _____

2. Mallory is considered a likely winner. _____

   _____

3. Ben gives great advice. _____

   _____

4. Lots of jokes were told by everyone in the group. _____

   _____

5. Serious issues were discussed in the presentation you missed. _____

   _____

C. Choose one topic and write four sentences about it. Use at least two active sentences and at least two passive sentences. Possible topics:

describe someone you'd like to be more like	a law you think should be passed	a second chance you'd like to have

1. _____

2. _____

3. _____

4. _____

Being a Freedom Rider

Use the graphic organizer below to make notes about the reasons to become a Freedom Rider, and the risks taken by Freedom Riders.

Sala Udin chose to become and remain a Freedom Rider, despite many dangers and his own personal experience.

Reasons to Become a Freedom Rider
_____
_____
_____
_____
_____
_____
_____
_____
_____
_____
_____
_____
_____

Risks Taken by Freedom Riders
_____
_____
_____
_____
_____
_____
_____
_____
_____
_____
_____
_____
_____

USE WHILE LISTENING TO THE PODCAST, AND WITH STUDENT BOOK pp. 106-107

Collaborative Discussion

What qualities do you think Sala Udin needed to be a Freedom Rider?

_____
_____
_____
_____
_____
_____
_____
_____
_____
_____

Which part of the story most shows the author's qualities? Explain.

_____
_____
_____
_____
_____
_____
_____
_____
_____
_____

Academic Vocabulary

A. Complete each sentence using a word from the box.

civil	civilian	civilizations	civil rights

1. If I am not in the military or the police, I am a _____ .

2. A _____ war takes place within a country.

3. Two great Asian _____ started thousands of years ago in China and India.

4. In 1964, President Lyndon Johnson signed the _____ Act, a law that gives all races of Americans equal rights.

B. Complete the answers with information from the text.

> In many early civilizations (the cities and states where people began to live in organized groups), powerful kings and their strong armies controlled the people. Often, ordinary civilians just worked and obeyed orders. Over the centuries, many civil wars have been fought when people wanted more rights and freedoms. One of the civil rights that people fought for was the right to vote and choose their leaders.

1. How were people controlled in early civilizations?

   In early civilizations, _____.

2. Who just worked and obeyed orders?

   _____ just worked and obeyed orders.

3. What kinds of wars were fought when people wanted more rights?

   _____ were fought when people wanted more rights and freedoms.

4. What is one of the civil rights people fought for?

   One of the civil rights that people fought for was _____.

C. Write a sentence or two about your favorite ancient or modern civilization, and tell why it interests you.

_____

_____

_____

Critical Vocabulary

A. Read the sentences below. Circle the definition of each underlined word. Remember that you can look up any unfamiliar words in the dictionary.

1. I feel <u>dread</u> about going outside when the weather is snowy and icy.

   a. fear   **b.** excited   **c.** eager

2. "Always <u>revere</u> your elders," my mother always tells me.

   a. respect   **b.** call   **c.** visit

3. I did not go to the party <u>solely</u> for the birthday cake, but I enjoyed eating it!

   a. always   **b.** often   **c.** only

4. Do you believe in the <u>existence</u> of life on other planets?

   a. suffering   **b.** presence   **c.** nightmare

B. Choose a word from the box to complete each sentence.

conformity	revere	dread	solely	mere	existence

1. Independent thinkers often do not enjoy living in societies that value _____.

2. Many people _____ having to make big changes in their lifestyle.

3. All of the team members _____ the coach and follow all of his advice.

4. The _____ presence of the movie star was enough to cause a traffic jam.

C. Choose two words from the box in Part B. Use each word in a sentence.

1. _____

   _____

   _____

   _____

2. _____

   _____

   _____

   _____

Homophones

A. Circle the homophone for each word.

1. our	owner	hour	over
2. great	grace	gate	grate
3. medal	mettle	needle	meal
4. sun	sunk	soon	son
5. flour	flower	flow	cloud

B. Complete the paragraph below by filling in each blank with the correct word from the box.

meddle	metal	our	hour	grate	great	son	sun

I hoped that my neighbor Rayna wouldn't _____ in the argument I was having with my

_____ , Nash. He is such a _____ kid, but sometimes he does things that

_____ on me like a squeaky _____ door. Nash likes to play loud music while at

the same time watching TV. Last night he did this for over an _____ while I was trying to

read. He insisted it wasn't loud. If I had not said something, I believe it would have continued until the

_____ rose the next morning. I'm glad we finally were able to resolve _____

argument.

C. Choose two homophone pairs from the box in Part B. Write a sentence using each word.

1. homophones: _____ and _____

_____

_____

2. homophones: _____ and _____

_____

_____

3. homophones: _____ and _____

_____

_____

4. homophones: _____ and _____

_____

_____

Collaborative Discussion

Each quote in this selection uses different words to convey a distinct message about freedom. Select four quotations to analyze. Summarize the message of the quotations in your own words, and discuss why the speaker's choice of words is clear and effective in conveying his or her thoughts.

Discussing the Purpose

First quote: _____

_____

What it means: _____

_____

Choice of words: _____

_____

Second quote: _____

_____

What it means: _____

_____

Choice of words: _____

Third quote: _____

What it means: _____

Choice of words: _____

Fourth quote: _____

What it means: _____

Choice of words: _____

Making Inferences

What does Medgar Evers's quote mean? _____

_____

Why might he have said this? _____

Write Your Ideas

Express your own ideas about freedom. Select a quotation that supports your ideas and include it in your paragraph. Remember to use the conventions for quotations highlighted in the Reading Toolbox on Student Book page 111.

What idea would I like to express about freedom? _____

_____

_____

_____

_____

_____

_____

_____

What quotation from the selection supports that idea? _____

_____

_____

_____

_____

_____

_____

_____

_____

Checklist:

	Does the quotation I chose support my main idea?
	Have I used quotation marks at the beginning of the quotation?
	Have I used quotation marks at the end of the quotation?
	Have I attributed the quotation properly?

Build Vocabulary

Metaphors

A. For each metaphor, identify the two things that are being compared.

1. education is the key

Two things being compared: _____

2. the golden door of freedom

Two things being compared: _____

3. conformity is the jailer of freedom

Two things being compared: _____

4. conformity is the enemy of freedom

Two things being compared: _____

B. Use the phrases from the box below to complete the sentences. Each sentence will contain at least one metaphor.

the daughter	the jailer	the golden door	the key	the enemy

1. For many individuals, a university degree is _____ that can unlock doors in many different fields.

2. My grandmother, who left China as a young woman, said the moment she arrived at

_____ of America was one of the happiest of her life.

3. Hatred is _____ of ignorance.

4. If you need to get up early, a book that you just can't put down is _____ .

5. Her shyness was _____ that kept her at home and stopped her from meeting new people.

C. Use three of the phrases from the box in Part B to write your own metaphors. Write a brief explanation of what each metaphor means on the lines provided.

Metaphor #1: _____

Meaning of this metaphor: _____

Metaphor #2: _____

Meaning of this metaphor: _____

Metaphor #3: _____

Meaning of this metaphor: _____

Indicative and Imperative Mood

A. **Determine whether the sentence is indicative or imperative. Circle the correct answer.**

1. Prepare for the storm by stocking up on groceries. [indicative, imperative]

2. I'll be collecting your tests at the end of three hours. [indicative, imperative]

3. Sharon doesn't like wearing turtlenecks. [indicative, imperative]

4. Be careful walking on the icy sidewalks. [indicative, imperative]

B. **Fill in the blank with an indicative or imperative verb that makes sense.**

1. _____ three spoonfuls of tea in that teapot.

2. I _____ more than a week to complete this assignment.

3. Please _____ your decision carefully.

4. Faith _____ beautiful poetry.

5. _____ about what you did!

C. **Choose one topic and write four sentences about it. Use at least two indicative sentences and at least two imperative sentences. Possible topics:**

make up a story about people resisting an unjust government	explain how to make a recipe	explain how to get to your favorite store

1. _____

_____

2. _____

_____

3. _____

_____

4. _____

_____

Build Vocabulary

Critical Vocabulary

A. Read the sentences below. Circle the definition of each underlined word. Remember that you can look up any unfamiliar words in the dictionary.

1. They were traveling by train, in the baggage car, protected by a <u>sympathetic</u> conductor.

    a. understanding   **b.** healthy   **c.** famous

2. When the band of <u>fugitives</u> finally reached Wilmington, the bridge over the Christiana River into the city was heavily guarded.

    a. spies   **b.** farmers   **c.** escapees

3. Everywhere they went, there were "wanted" posters with Joe's <u>likeness</u> on them.

    a. dog   **b.** picture   **c.** description

4. Joe Bailey had been a great help to Tubman all along the way, but when they reached New York City, he began to <u>despair</u>.

    a. become weak   **b.** lose hope   **c.** talk

B. Choose a word from the box to complete each sentence.

bounty	likeness	sympathetic	fugitives	despair	retorted

1. When the government wants to catch an important criminal, they print up a "Wanted" poster with the person's description and _____ on it.

2. Some people earn money by catching _____ from the law.

3. When they capture a wanted person, the government pays them the amount of the _____ that they had advertised.

4. I asked the man why he did such dangerous work, and he _____ that it paid really well.

C. Choose two words from the box in Part B. Use each word in a sentence. Write the sentence.

1. _____

_____

_____

2. _____

_____

_____

Academic Vocabulary

A. Complete each sentence with the correct word from the box.

demonstrate	demonstrable

1. The band will _____ what goes into making a hit record.

demonstration	demonstrated

2. When the mayor told the townspeople they would have to pay for the water they use, they organized a _____ .

demonstrate	demonstration

3. The saleswoman offered to give us a _____ of the new technology.

demonstrable	demonstrate

4. This project has no _____ connection to the subject we're studying.

B. Complete each sentence.

1. The good grade on my test demonstrates _____.

2. We want to have a organize a demonstration because _____.

C. Using one of the words in the box, write a sentence about a cause that might inspire someone to go to a demonstration.

demonstrate	demonstration

_____

_____

128 USE WITH LESSON 16.3

Analyzing the Text

Use this page to make notes about the questions in the Analyzing the Text section on page 116 in the Student Book.

Why do you think the author began the selection by telling the price Joe Bailey's owner paid for him?

_____

_____

Why was Joe so discouraged toward the end of the journey?

_____

_____

What does the author explicitly say in the text?

_____

_____

_____

_____

_____

_____

_____

_____

_____

What can be inferred from the information she provided?

_____

_____

_____

_____

_____

_____

_____

_____

_____

Practice and Apply

Use this page to make an outline summarizing the main ideas of "Joe Bailey's Freedom."
Fill in only the parts you need.

I. _____
_____

   A. _____

   B. _____

II. _____
_____

   A. _____

   B. _____

III. _____
_____

   A. _____

   B. _____

IV. _____
_____

   A. _____

   B. _____

V. _____
_____

   A. _____

   B. _____

VI. _____
_____

   A. _____

   B. _____

Compound Words

A. Choose a word from the box below to answer each question.

| underground | railroad | overseer | rowboat | bricklayer | cartload | everywhere |

1. What word describes an individual who supervises or watches over the work of others?

_____

2. What word describes an individual who uses bricks to build structures? _____

3. What word implies that something can be found in all places or all over? _____

4. What word can be used to indicate that something is hidden from plain sight?

_____

5. What word describes a permanent track constructed specifically for locomotives?

_____

6. What word refers to the amount of something that can fit inside a cart? _____

B. Complete each sentence with a word from the box in Part A.

1. The _____ of the plantation was known for being a cruel man who gave his workers few breaks.

2. It is difficult to save money when advertisements for products seem to be _____ you look.

3. We grabbed the oars of the _____ and quickly began to move away from shore.

4. The horses strained to pull the heavy _____ of bricks up the steep hill.

5. There is an exciting _____ movie scene set in a part of the country that few are aware even exists.

C. Choose three compound words from the box in Part A. Use each word in a sentence. Underline the compound word in each sentence.

1. _____

_____

2. _____

_____

3. _____

_____

Analyze the Text

Compare the actions of Harriet Tubman and the Underground Railroad to those of the Muslims in *The Grand Mosque of Paris.*

Kabyle Resistance	**Underground Railroad**

Who were they?

Who did they help?

How did they help?

USE WITH STUDENT BOOK p. 117

© Houghton Mifflin Harcourt Publishing Company

Write an Outline

Read the assignment in the Performance Task section of Student Book page 117 to complete this task.

What?	
What was the event? What happened during the event?	

Who?	
Who was involved in the event?	

Where?	
Where did the event take place?	

When?	
When did the event occur? Over what time period?	

Why?	
Why was the event significant or noteworthy?	

Specialized Vocabulary

A. Choose the correct words from the box below to answer each question.

plantation	fugitives	slave	bounty	abolitionist	freedom

1. What term describes a person who is considered to be the property of another individual?

   _____

2. What did those who traveled on the Underground Railroad hope to find in their new home?

   _____

3. What term refers to a large farm often found in a warm climate that produces crops such as cotton

   and coffee? _____

4. What was the reward offered for the return of escaped slaves called? _____

5. What term describes "runaway slaves" who left their "master's" homes without permission to seek

   out better lives? _____

6. What is the title for a person who opposes slavery and wants to see the practice ended?

   _____

B. Complete each sentence with the correct word from the box. Each term will only be used once.

1. Harriet Tubman was a famous _____ who risked her life to lead runaway slaves

   to freedom.

2. Being a _____ meant not having any of the rights and privileges people in

   America today take for granted.

3. Furious that one of his slaves had run away, the cruel "master" decided to put a

   _____ on the slave's head.

4. The fields of the _____ were lined with laborers who stood sweating in the

   heat as they pulled cotton from the bushes.

5. The _____ traveled by darkness after they escaped to avoid being captured

   and returned to their "owner."

C. Write a sentence using three of the terms from the box in Part A. Underline the term in
each sentence. Each sentence should contain a different term.

1. _____

2. _____

3. _____

Critical Vocabulary

A. Read the sentences below. Circle the definition of each underlined word. Remember that you can look up any unfamiliar words in the dictionary.

1. In 1977, two *Voyager* spacecraft <u>were launched</u> from Cape Canaveral, Florida.

   a. built   **b.** blasted off   **c.** taken away

2. These spacecraft have accomplished an enormous amount during their <u>extended</u> mission.

   a. lengthened   **b.** exciting   **c.** dangerous

3. Beyond Earth's atmosphere and its gravitational pull, objects are free to move with very little <u>resistance</u>.

   a. opposing force   **b.** alien armies   **c.** heat overflow

4. The size of the craft matters less than its <u>velocity</u>.

   a. length   **b.** speed   **c.** coating of paint

B. Choose a word from the box to complete each sentence.

launched	solar system	extended	sketches	resistance	velocity

1. We live in a _____, and we know that ours is not the only one.

2. The artist made quick _____ of all the students in the class.

3. Because of the snowstorm, school vacation was _____ a few extra days.

4. With modern technology, we can measure the _____ of baseball pitchers' fastballs.

C. Choose three words from the box in Part B. Use each word in a sentence.

1. _____

   _____

2. _____

   _____

3. _____

   _____

Interrogative Mood

(Hint: Helping verb + subject + main verb + rest of sentence)

A. Determine how to restructure the indicative sentence to make it interrogative. Circle the correct answer.

1. I stretched before running.

   a. Did I stretch before running?　　**b.** Stretched I before running?

2. Mikki baked brownies.

   a. Did Mikki baked brownies?　　**b.** What did Mikki bake?

3. Jake works in an office.

   a. Is Jake work in an office?　　**b.** Does Jake work in an office?

4. We trust her because she wears her heart on her sleeve.

   a. Why do we trust her?　　**b.** What do we trust her?

B. Fill in the blank with a helping verb that makes sense.

1. _____ Jay going on the trip next week?

2. Who _____ bring snacks?

3. _____ Nicholas tell you that?

4. Where _____ you been all day?

5. _____ anyone actually want this dessert?

C. Choose one topic and write four sentences about it. Use at least two interrogative sentences. Possible topics:

a debate between two fictional characters	a teacher explaining something	a short piece explaining your opinion on something important

1. _____

2. _____

3. _____

4. _____

Academic Vocabulary

A. Complete each sentence with the correct word from the box.

document	documentation

1. People collected photographs and posters to _____ the demonstrations.

documentary	document

2. Some _____ filmmakers want to inform people about some terrible thing that has happened.

documents	documentary

3. The judge demanded to see all of the _____ related to the case.

documentation	documentary

4. If you own a house, it's important to keep all of the ownership _____ in a safe place.

B. Read the passage and answer the questions.

> When U.S. presidents leave office, they donate many of their personal documents to their presidential libraries. These libraries provide documentation for historians to study. Presidents and their staffs often keep diaries to help document how decisions were made. There may be a theater where documentaries are shown in the library.

1. What do presidents donate to their presidential libraries?

They donate _____.

2. Why do historians use these libraries?

The libraries provide _____.

3. What do the presidential staff's diaries document?

The diaries document _____.

4. What are the theaters for in these libraries?

The libraries have theaters _____.

C. Using a word from the box, write a sentence about something a historian could use to document your life.

document	documents	documentation

_____

Critical Vocabulary

A. Read the sentences below. Circle the definition of each underlined word. Remember that you can look up any unfamiliar words in the dictionary.

1. Caderousse <u>resents</u> Dante love of life. *Resents* means

   a. dislikes.   **b.** appreciates.   **c.** confuses.

2. A captain at his age? I <u>deserve</u> that post. *Deserve* means

   a. hate.   **b.** understand.   **c.** should have.

3. The <u>treasure</u> on the island of Monte Cristo is beyond belief. *Treasure* means

   a. bad luck.   **b.** riches.   **c.** friendship.

4 The "friends" write a letter accusing Dante of <u>treason</u>. *Treason* means

   a. rules.   **b.** disloyalty.   **c.** anger.

B. Choose a word from the box to complete each sentence.

deserve	resents	treason	fortune	professional	shroud

1. It was said that the ancient shipwreck had buried a _____ of gold and silver at the bottom of the sea.

2. He had the ambitious dream of becoming a _____ basketball player.

3. The mountain was hidden under a _____ of mist.

4. I have been working hard all morning so I _____ a break.

C. Choose three words from the box in Part B. Use each word in a sentence.

1. _____

   _____

2. _____

   _____

3. _____

   _____

The Vocabulary of Revenge

A. Choose the correct words from the box below to answer each question.

accuse	avenge	betray	charges	enemy
jealous	revenge	ruin	to make amends	treason

1. What term describes a feeling of resentment related to another person's job, money, success, etc.?

_____

2. What term describes the crime of trying to bring down the government? _____

3. What term is a synonym for "downfall" or "destruction"? _____

4. What term refers to formal accusations, especially those made against someone believed to have

broken the law? _____

5. What term means "to be disloyal" or "to deceive"? _____

6. What term describes the act of seeking revenge on behalf of another person who was wronged?

_____

B. Complete each sentence with the correct word from the box in Part A.
Each term will only be used once.

1. I tried _____ for missing his birthday party by giving him the most valuable
graphic novel in my collection.

2. Most people take great offense when others _____ them of things they did not do.

3. We were once the best of friends, but he became my bitter _____ after we had a huge
disagreement last year.

4. The main character of the novel vowed to take _____ against those who caused him to
lose his job and his family.

5. I never thought she would _____ me, so I was shocked when I learned she had been
stealing from me for months.

C. Choose three terms from the box in Part A. Write a sentence using each term.
Underline the term in each sentence.

1. _____

2. _____

3. _____

Information in a Graphic Novel

Read the directions in the Performance Task section on page 130 of the Student Book to complete this page.

Onomatopoeia

A. Match the sounds in the box below to the most likely source of each sound.

bzzzzzzz	woof	splat	pow	clap
ding	boing	sshhh	zzzzzz	quack

1. a bee _____

2. a sleeping tiger _____

3. a pair of hands _____

4. a dog _____

5. a ball _____

6. a duck _____

7. a bell _____

B. Write the sound from the box in Part A that most closely fits each of the following descriptions of illustrations. None of the sounds will be used more than once.

1. Two students sit at a table in a library leaned close to each other. A librarian is standing in front of the table with a stern look on her face. She is holding her index finger in front of her lips. _____

2. A woman is standing to the side of a large punching bag. She is crouched low, and her arm is extended. Her fist is the bag. _____

3. A large hive is attached to a tree. There are a number of insects flying around the hive. _____

4. A child stands on a sidewalk holding on upside-down ice cream cone. The scoop of ice cream that was inside the cone is now on top of the sidewalk. _____

5. A tennis player stands with a racket in his right hand. His left hand is held out to his side, ready to catch the ball he just bounced off the court. _____

C. Choose four examples of onomatopoeia from the box in Part A. Use each example in a sentence. Underline the example of onomatopoeia in each sentence.

1. _____

2. _____

3. _____

4. _____

Conditional and Subjunctive Mood

A. Decide whether the underlined verb is in the conditional or subjunctive mood. Circle the correct answer.

1. When we first met, I wished I <u>were</u> more impressive. [conditional, subjunctive]

2. If I felt sick, I <u>would</u> go to the doctor. [conditional, subjunctive]

3. If you would help her, Amal <u>could finish</u> in time. [conditional, subjunctive]

4. Andrea suggested that Mia <u>study</u> with her. [conditional, subjunctive]

B. Fill in the blank with a conditional or subjunctive verb that makes sense.

1. If you _____ me what I missed, that would be really helpful.

2. This professor asks that students _____ their notes to class.

3. I would enjoy plane rides if only takeoff _____ less scary.

4. If we went home early, we _____ a lot of important information.

5. Most people _____ a lot healthier if they could cook at home more often.

C. Choose one topic and write four sentences about it. Use at least one conditional verb and at least one subjunctive verb. Possible topics:

what you'd like to do in college	what you would do if you could fly	what you would change about yourself if you could shapeshift

1. _____

_____

2. _____

_____

3. _____

_____

4. _____

_____

Speak Out!

Make notes about the Speak Out! question.

What did Dantes's friends do to him?

_____

_____

_____

Was Dantes right to feel betrayed and angry? Explain.

_____

_____

_____

Dantes forgave Caderousse because he said he was sorry and ashamed. Did Dantes give the other men the chance to do that?

_____

_____

_____

Did Mondego and Danglars deserve what he did to them?

_____

_____

_____

Did Dantes hurt any innocent people? Explain.

_____

_____

_____

Do you think Dantes's actions made him as bad as Mondego and Danglars?

_____

_____

_____

_____

Build Vocabulary

Irregular Comparative and Superlative Forms

A. For each word below, write the comparative and the superlative form.

Word	Comparative	Superlative
good		
many		
little		
far		
bad		

B. Complete the sentences with the words from the table in Part A. For each sentence, identify the best adjective or adverb from the table and the correct form of the word.

1. Of the dozens of mistakes I've made during my life, lying to my best friend has to be the _____ .

2. Many people are upset about the construction of the new highway, but I think it is a _____ thing.

3. The town of Springdale is _____ away from my house than the city of Brightbridge is.

4. It is never a good idea to talk about people behind their backs, but writing mean things about them online is even _____ .

5. Because I practiced hard all season, I scored the _____ points ever during our final hockey game.

6. My small glass can hold much _____ water than a large juice pitcher can.

7. There are so _____ reasons why I believe cats make better pets than dogs that it's impossible to list them all.

C. Choose a word from the table in Part A and use the word to write three sentences. Each sentence should use a different form of the word.

Word: _____

Sentence #1: _____

_____

Sentence #2: _____

_____

Sentence #3: _____

_____

Informative Essay

A. Here is a list of the reading and podcast selections from this unit. Pick three of the selections and describe the main idea of each one you choose.

"Every Blog Has Its Day"

from The Grand Mosque of Paris

"I Want to Be a Freedom Writer"

"Talking About Freedom"

"Joe Bailey's Freedom"

"Escaping Earth"

"The Count of Monte Cristo"

_____

_____

_____

B. Write three possible main ideas for your essay.

Idea 1 _____

_____

_____

Idea 2 _____

_____

_____

Idea 3 _____

_____

_____

Plan Your Essay

To evaluate your essay, use the Informative Essay Rubric available from your online Student Resources or from your teacher.

Main Idea

Write your main idea. Remember, you can use a statement or a question. You may also include an interesting quote from one of the selections.

_____

_____

Supporting Details

What details will support your main idea?

_____

_____

What evidence from the texts can you use?

_____

_____

What other sources can you use to find details?

_____

_____

Vocabulary

Are there any proper nouns that you may need to explain?

_____

_____

Text Features

What are some ideas for the title of your essay?

_____

_____

What subheads will you use in your essay? Remember, subheads are needed if your supporting details can be grouped together.

_____

_____

Academic Vocabulary

A. Complete each sentence with the correct word from the box.

symbolism	symbolized

1. In the Chinese calendar, every year is _____ by an animal.

symbol	symbolism

2. ☺ is an easy-to-understand _____.

symbolism	symbolic

3. Apple pie is _____ of the United States.

symbolizes	symbolism

4. The Statue of Liberty _____ freedom to many immigrants.

B. Complete each sentence.

1. If I had to choose one object that would symbolize me, it would be _____ because

_____.

2. I use symbols when I _____

_____.

C. A particular building or landform often symbolizes a city or state. Using one of the words from the box, write a sentence about something that would symbolize your city or town.

symbol	symbolize	symbolic	symbolism

_____

_____

_____

Finalize Your Plan

WRITING TOOLBOX

Elements of an Informative Essay

Opening Paragraph	Present your main idea. Include an interesting fact, question, or quotation.
Supporting Detail	Each paragraph should include a supporting detail to support your main idea. You may want to use subheads to group your ideas.
Conclusion	The conclusion should sum up how the details support your main idea. You may want to include a question to make the reader think.

A. Review the elements of an informative essay above. Describe the elements that you will include in your essay.

Opening Paragraph _____

_____

_____

Supporting Details _____

_____

_____

Conclusion _____

_____

_____

B. Write a brief summary of your essay.

_____

_____

_____

_____

Vocabulary Review

Here are some of the words you learned in this unit. Choose words from this list and sort them into the categories below. There are many possible correct answers!

accessibility	century	injustice	shhh
accessible	civilization	network	subterranean
afford	clandestine	obedience	symbol
avenge	code	overseer	symbolism
boing	conformity	percentage	terrain
bounty	demonstration	pow	terrarium
bricklayer	ding	property	terrestrial
bzzzzz	documentary	railroad	treason
cartload	everywhere	rough	underground
centenarian	excuse	rowboat	woof
centimeter	extravagant	splat	

Words with the Root *terr*

1. _____
2. _____
3. _____
4. _____
5. _____

Compound Words

1. _____
2. _____
3. _____
4. _____
5. _____

Words with the Root *cent*

1. _____
2. _____
3. _____
4. _____
5. _____

Onomatopoeia

1. _____
2. _____
3. _____
4. _____
5. _____

Easily Confused Words

A. Circle the correct word in each sentence. Use the context clues to help you decide.

1. There will be a half-hour [wait, weight] before we can get in to the concert.

2. I'm having trouble gaining back the [wait, weight] I lost when I was sick.

3. Take a deep [breath, breathe] before you do something rash.

4. Even if you [belief, believe] in yourself, you have to recognize your own limits.

B. Fill in the blanks with the correct word that fits in the context of the sentence.

1. This storm is shaking my _____ that I can wear t-shirts in all weather.

2. Kim's nose is so blocked up that she has to _____ through her mouth.

3. Can you _____ until we get home?

4. Are you sure you fully understand the _____ of this decision?

5. Lisa, I _____ it's your turn next.

C. Write four sentences, one using *wait*, one using *weight*, one using *breathe* or *breath*, and one using *belief* or *believe*. Your sentences should demonstrate your understanding of the meaning of each word.

1. _____

_____

_____

2. _____

_____

_____

3. _____

_____

_____

4. _____

_____

_____

Approaching Adulthood

"Growth is life, and life is forever destined to make for light."

—Jack London, writer

What do you think of when you hear the word "adolescence"? Make visual or written notes.

When you are an adolescent, what can you look forward to?

_____

_____

What are you trying to hold onto?

_____

_____

Name two things that are really important to teenagers.

_____

_____

Name one thing that you think will be important when you're an adult.

_____

_____

Academic Vocabulary

As you work through Unit 4 look and listen for these words. Practice using them when you talk in class and in your writing. Write about your experiences using these words in the last column of the chart.

Word	Definition	Related Forms	My Experiences
debate	• to discuss or argue different opinions • a discussion about different opinions	debatable	
deduce	to reach a conclusion or decision through reasoning	deduction, deductive	
license	• to give official permission • an official document that gives someone permission	licensed	
sufficient	enough	sufficiently, insufficient, self-sufficient	
trend	• the general direction of change • a current style	trendy, trendsetter	

Word Timeline

Use the column on the right to write the meanings of the words in the column on the left.

Word	Meaning
fatherhood	
priesthood	
statehood	
darkness	
happiness	
friendship	
citizenship	
ownership	
annoyance	
absence	
independence	

Word Timeline

Follow the directions in the Performance Task on page 139 of the Student Book to complete this task.

Write down words for different ages.

Formal	Informal
_____	_____
_____	_____
_____	_____
_____	_____
_____	_____
_____	_____
_____	_____
_____	_____
_____	_____

Use the line below to make your Word Timeline.

Formal

Informal

Discuss the Purpose

Read Student Book pp. 140–142 to complete this page.

1. Does Placido look forward to being an adult?

_____

_____

2. What are two specific things he mentions not liking?

_____

_____

3. What adjectives could you use to describe the picture of being an adult that Placido draws in that entry?

_____

_____

4. What adjectives could you use to describe Placido's attitude?

_____

_____

Changes in Placido's attitude:

5. What changes Placido's attitude?

_____

_____

6. What advice does his brother give him?

_____

_____

7. What is Placido most worried about in the later blog entry?

_____

_____

8. Does Placido say that he agrees with his brother? Do you think he does? Explain.

_____

_____

Critical Vocabulary

A. Read the sentences below. Circle the definition of each underlined word.
Remember that you can look up any unfamiliar words in the dictionary.

1. Summer <u>precedes</u> autumn. *Precedes* means

   a. comes before.   **b.** comes after.   **c.** delays.

2. Placido wants to start <u>managing</u> his money well. *Managing* means

   a. making.   **b.** handling.   **c.** counting.

3. Adulthood means working and wearing <u>sensible</u> shoes. *Sensible* means

   a. fancy.   **b.** practical.   **c.** boring.

4. He decided to act like a big brother, which was an unusual <u>occurrence</u>. An *occurrence* is

   a. an incident.   **b.** an accident.   **c.** a coincidence.

B. Choose a word from the box to complete each sentence.

precedes	occurrence	managing	approach
sensible	humored	achieve	tut-tut

1. You can _____ your goals while still having fun.

2. The adults _____ in disapproval as they read the newspaper.

3. I _____ my brother's silly questions and answered each one.

4. When teenagers _____ adulthood, they accept more responsibility.

5. He is _____ his money by saving a portion of his check.

C. Choose three words from the box in Part B. Use each word in a sentence.

1. _____

   _____

2. _____

   _____

3. _____

   _____

Schedule a Blog Calendar

Read the Performance Task on page 142 of the Student Book to complete this task. Don't forget to check the Blog Rubric, available from your online Student Resources or from your teacher.

Movie Recommendation

Movie title:

_____

What I liked:

_____

_____

_____

Reminder of an Event

Event:

_____

Date:

_____

Place:

_____

Time:

_____

Celebrating a Holiday

Holiday:

_____

Date:

_____

Design:

_____

_____

_____

Multiple-Meaning Words

A. Choose the word from the box that most closely fits each of the following definitions.

type	entry	lean	clear	sensible	honey

1. This word can refer to a sweet fluid produced by bees. It can also be an affectionate name for a loved one. _____

2. This word can be used to describe the act of resting against something. It can also mean "thin" or "having just a little fat." _____

3. This word can describe a group that consists of members with similar characteristics. It can also refer to the print found in texts such as newspapers and books. _____

4. This word can describe an item or "chunk" of information that is written down (e.g., a dictionary entry). It can also refer to the opening that allows a person to go into a building. _____

5. This word can be used to indicate that something is easy to see. It can also indicate that something is easy to understand. _____

6. This word can indicate that something is practical or durable. It can also be used to indicate that an individual has good sense and/or displays sound judgment. _____

B. For each sentence, write the definition of the underlined word on the line provided. Use the definitions provided in Part A to help you complete this section.

1. Although my grandmother rarely eats sugar, she always puts a drop of <u>honey</u> into her morning tea.

   _____

2. My neighbor says she trusts me to babysit her son because I am a <u>sensible</u> young woman.

   _____

3. After a summer of working long hours on a farm, he was tanned and <u>lean</u>.

   _____

4. We were able to put the desk together in no time at all thanks to the <u>clear</u> instructions that described each step. _____

5. The <u>type</u> on the webpage was so tiny I had to squint to read it. _____

   _____

C. Choose a multiple-meaning word from the box in Part A. Write two sentences using the word. Underline the word in each sentence. The word should have a different meaning in each sentence. Multiple Meaning Word: _____

Sentence 1: _____

Sentence 2: _____

Adjectives

A. Determine what kind of adjective the underlined word is. Circle the correct answer.

1. I think this milk has gone <u>bad</u>

    a. article   **b.** size   **c.** subject complement   **d.** quantitative

2. Jean saw her grandmother the <u>other</u> day.

    a. descriptive   **b.** quantitative   **c.** opinion   **d.** material

3. I waited for you for <u>two</u> hours!

    a. subject complement   **b.** article   **c.** age   **d.** quantitative

4. This painting is <u>the</u> pride of the museum's collection

    a. descriptive   **b.** color   **c.** subject complement   **d.** article

B. Fill in the blank with at least two adjectives.

1. We recently adopted _____ dog.

2. _____ musician is coming to San Francisco soon.

3. These _____ stairs take caution to navigate.

4. I make _____ decisions with input from my family.

5. This song is _____ hit!

C. Choose one topic and write four sentences about it. Use at least one adjective per sentence and use multiple adjectives for one noun at least twice. Possible topics:

what makes a good neighbor	your favorite time of day	something that really bugs you

1. _____

    _____

2. _____

    _____

3. _____

    _____

4. _____

    _____

Persuasion

Answer the questions about *Rocker Girl*.

1. Why is Alex at the counselor's office?

_____

_____

2. Why does Alex think she doesn't need school?

_____

_____

3. What evidence does Alex present to try to persuade the counselor that she is doing what's best for

her future career? _____

_____

_____

4. What kind of work does the counselor say Alex will have to do if she gets to be successful?

_____

_____

5. What does Alex say she knows how to do because she learned it at school?

_____

_____

6. What does the counselor suggest Alex could study in college?

_____

_____

Compare and Contrast

Think about the video you have just seen. Compare and contrast it with "Placido's Place."

1. What common topic do the video and the blog share?

_____

_____

2. What difference do you see between the video and the blog? _____

_____

_____

3. What point of view, if any, is closer to yours? Explain.

_____

_____

Critical Vocabulary

A. Circle four words in the Word Bank that you want to know more about.

Word Bank					
trend	convince	succeed	locate	promote	contracts
venues	manager	survive	lawyer	destiny	marketing

B. Watch the video *Rocker Girl* again and listen for the words. Complete the activity.

1. Word: _____

What I think it means: _____

What it means: _____

2. Word: _____

What I think it means: _____

What it means: _____

3. Word: _____

What I think it means: _____

What it means: _____

4. Word: _____

What I think it means: _____

What it means: _____

C. Choose three words that you wrote in Part B. Write a sentence using each word.

1. _____

_____

2. _____

_____

3. _____

_____

Academic Vocabulary

A. Read the passage and answer the questions.

> Some politicians say that the benefits of recess in middle school are debatable.
> The debate over the value of recess began when legislators complained that recess is
> a waste of time, and students should be learning. Psychologists are quick to debate
> the issue because they believe that students pay more attention after a break.

1. What do some politicians say about the benefits of recess?

They say that the benefits _____.

2. When did the debate about recess begin?

The debate began _____.

3. What were psychologists quick to do?

Psychologists were quick to _____.

B. Complete each sentence, underlining your choice of verb in Question 2.

1. If I organized a debate, it would be about _____

_____.

2. I enjoy/do not enjoy debating because _____

_____.

C. Some stores open on Thanksgiving because that's what shoppers want. Other stores close
to let their employees celebrate the holiday with their families. Using a form of *debate* or
debatable, write a sentence or two explaining your opinion about this debate.

_____

_____

_____

_____

_____

_____

_____

_____

Critical Vocabulary

A. Read the sentences below. Circle the definition of each underlined word. Remember that you can look up any unfamiliar words in the dictionary.

1. The color of the doll's hair and dress matched my own, but I didn't feel as <u>elegant</u> as she looked. *Elegant* means

    a. refined.   **b.** miniature   **c.** fake.

2. It wasn't only my feet though, that <u>lacked</u> elegance. *Lacked* means

    a. is missing.   **b.** has an abundance of   **c.** owns.

3. I <u>glimpsed</u> Abuela leaning back in her chair. *Glimpsed* means

    a. looked briefly at.   **b.** investigated.   **c.** looked long and hard at.

4. On top of my cake sat a <u>figurine</u> of a woman with black hair. A *figurine* is

    a. a type of candle.   **b.** a small figure.   **c.** a type of dessert.

B. Choose a word from the box to complete each sentence.

elegant	gratitude	flocked	matched
saddle	lacked	figurine	glimpse

1. I learned how to _____ a horse at the ranch.

2. I'm filled with _____ when I think about how supportive my family is.

3. We _____ to the banquet hall with the rest of the guests.

4. From the corner of my eye, I could _____ my grandparents watching me dance.

5. My dress _____ the color of my eyes.

C. Choose three words from the box in Part B. Use each word in a sentence.

1. _____

   _____

2. _____

   _____

3. _____

   _____

Write a Narrative

When you write your short narrative, remember that you can use events that happened to you or to someone you know—or you can make up the entire story. Read page 149 of the Student Book to complete this page.

Characters Who are the important characters in your story?	_____ _____ _____ _____ _____
Setting Where does the birthday celebration happen? When does it happen?	_____ _____ _____ _____ _____
Plot What happens?	_____ _____ _____ _____ _____
Narrator Who will tell the story?	_____ _____ _____ _____ _____

Homophones

A. Use the homophone pairs in the box below to answer the questions.

wrapping/rapping	cell/sell	heard/herd	right/write
then/than	course/coarse	real/reel	

1. Which word is used to draw a comparison between two things? _____

2. Which word means "correct"? _____

3. Which word indicates that something actually exists? _____

4. Which word describes something that has a rough texture? _____

5. Which word can be used as a synonym for "thumping" or "knocking"? _____

6. Which word indicates that something was perceived by the ear? _____

B. Use the homophone pairs in the box in Part A to complete the sentences.

1. I spotted a large _____ of cattle in a farmer's field as we were driving along the country road.

2. Since my bicycle was too small for me, I decided to _____ it to a kid in my neighborhood.

3. She ate her breakfast, and _____ she headed out the door to catch the school bus.

4. One of the best tips I ever got for staying organized is to _____ down exactly what I need to do each day.

5. The theater worker put the film _____ into the projector and watched as the moving images began to dance across the large screen.

C. Choose two homophone pairs from the box in Part A. Write a sentence using each word. Underline the homophone in each sentence.

1. Homophones: _____ and _____

Sentence 1: _____

Sentence 2: _____

2. Homophones: _____ and _____

Sentence 1: _____

Sentence 2: _____

Critical Vocabulary

A. Read the sentences below. Circle the definition of each underlined word. Remember that you can look up any unfamiliar words in the dictionary.

1. All presidents have their own particular interests and <u>aversions</u>. *Aversions* are

   a. strong dislikes.   **b.** passions.   **c.** hobbies.

2. Andrew Johnson gained a lot of skills from his <u>challenging</u> background. *Challenging* means

   a. simple.   **b.** difficult.   **c.** fun.

3. Teddy Roosevelt took steps to preserve the country's natural wonders for the <u>benefit</u> of future generations. *Benefit* means

   a. legacy.   **b.** advantage.   **c.** disadvantage.

4. The <u>enthusiastic</u> nature-lover went on to become a powerful conservationist. *Enthusiastic* means

   a. passionate.   **b.** frenzied   **c.** honest.

B. Choose a word from the box to complete each sentence.

aversions	deficits	challenging	enthusiastic
privilege	apprenticed	elected	benefit

1. It is a _____ to be the president of the United States.

2. Reading a biography of a former president is a good way to learn both the accomplishments and _____ of their term.

3. Presidents are always _____ by the majority.

4. Some presidents were _____ in order to learn a trade.

5. The _____ reader will be very excited to visit the presidential library.

C. Choose three words from the box in Part B. Use each word in a sentence.

1. _____

   _____

2. _____

   _____

3. _____

   _____

Participles

A. Determine whether the participle in the sentence modifies the subject, the subject complement, the direct object, or the object of a preposition. Circle the correct answer.

1. Driving home, I thought of a tricky problem.

    a. subject   **b.** subject complement

    c. direct object   **d.** object of a preposition

2. The interviewer asked many interesting questions.

    a. subject   **b.** subject complement

    c. direct object   **d.** object of a preposition

3. This novel is a beloved bestseller.

    a. subject   **b.** subject complement

    c. direct object   **d.** object of a preposition

4. I slowly opened the door to the forbidden chamber.

    a. subject   **b.** subject complement

    c. direct object   **d.** object of a preposition

B. Fill in the blank with a participle that makes sense.

1. The _____ listeners paid close attention.

2. Eric was a _____ mess.

3. I took the files out of the _____ box.

4. Is the _____ phone yours?

5. Linda ate some _____ potatoes.

C. Choose one topic and write a paragraph about it. Use at least four participles in your paragraph. Possible topics:

describe someone who has had an important effect on you.	explain how to deal with someone who bothers you	what it would be like to live underwater

_____

_____

_____

_____

_____

Compare and Contrast Presidents

President	Rich or Poor?	Worked when young?	Went to school?
John Quincy Adams			
Abraham Lincoln			
Andrew Johnson			
Teddy Roosevelt			

USE WITH STUDENT BOOK pp. 151–154

© Houghton Mifflin Harcourt Publishing Company

Analyze the Text

Use Student Book p. 154 and the selection to answer the questions below.

1. Andrew Johnson

Summarize what the author explicitly says about Andrew Johnson.

_____

_____

_____

How might his background have helped him as president?

_____

_____

_____

How might his background have hurt him?

_____

_____

_____

2. John Quincy Adams

How did John Quincy Adams's experience as the son of a president help him to become president?
Use the text as well as inference to help you answer.

What does the text say directly?

_____

_____

_____

What can you infer?

_____

_____

_____

Academic Vocabulary

A. Complete each sentence with the correct word from the box.

deduce	deduction	deductive

1. One of the investigative techniques used by detectives is _____ reasoning.
2. I can _____ from the stroller and the toys in the yard that young children live in this house.
3. Sherlock Holmes found a number of clues, and based on these he made a _____.

B. Read the passage and answer the questions.

> The detective used deductive reasoning to solve the crime. First she said, "Valuable things are missing, and the owner was not home, so they must have been stolen." Then she deduced that this was correct by finding clues about where and how the thief got in. Her final deduction was that the thief cut a hole in the screen and climbed through the open window.

1. What did the detective use to solve the crime?
   She used _____.
2. What evidence did she look for to deduce this?
   She deduced it by finding _____.
3. What was her final deduction?
   Her final deduction was _____
   _____.

C. Using one of the words from the box, write a sentence about what you might deduce about a man wearing work boots and a hard hat.

_____
_____
_____
_____
_____
_____

Antonyms

Use the graphic organizer to help you determine the meanings of the targeted words.

Future presidents grew up like other children of
their times, in all kinds of family situations, with
individual gifts and deficits, interests and aversions,
challenges and opportunities.

gifts and deficits

In this context, what is the meaning
of the word *gifts*?

_____

_____

_____

What is the meaning of the
word *deficits*?

_____

_____

_____

What is another antonym for *gifts*?

_____

_____

_____

interests and aversions

In this context, what is the meaning
of the word *interests*?

_____

_____

_____

What is the meaning of the
word *aversions*?

_____

_____

_____

What is another antonym for *interests*?

_____

_____

_____

Linguistic Context Clues: Antonyms

A. Read the sentence below and then answer the questions that follow.

> Abraham Lincoln was a self-educated man, not like our country's more recent presidents, who have been educated in institutions.

1. What are the two antonyms in the sentence? _____

2. What context clue suggests these two terms are antonyms? _____

3. Can you think of a way to rewrite the sentence using a different context clue to contrast the two antonyms? Your new sentence should have the same meaning and include the two antonyms found in the original.

   _____

B. For each sentence, circle the word that would be best to write on the line. Each completed sentence will contrast two antonyms. Then identify the two antonyms in the completed sentence.

1. Some people adore classical music, _____ I absolutely loathe it.

   but   not like   unlike

   antonyms: _____

2. _____ I felt encouraged when so many people signed up for the fundraising event, I was disheartened by the fact that hardly anyone actually showed up.

   Unlike   Instead of   While

   antonyms: _____

3. She has a self-assured demeanor that is completely _____ my timid manner.

   although   unlike   instead of

   antonyms: _____

4. _____ always being a pessimist, why don't you try to be more of an optimist like me?

   Instead of   But   Not like

   antonyms: _____

C. Write two sentences that use "either...or," "while," and "although" to contrast two antonyms. Underline the antonyms in each sentence.

1. _____

2. _____

Sequence of Events

Fill in the chart to indicate the sequence of events in "The Fir Tree." When you're finished, compare what you've written with the chart on Student Book page 157.

Collaborative Discussion

Do you notice any patterns in the life of the young fir tree?

_____

_____

_____

_____

_____

_____

_____

_____

What is the lesson the tree learns at the end of the story?

_____

_____

_____

_____

_____

_____

_____

_____

_____

How does this lesson apply to people's experience as they grow up?

_____

_____

_____

_____

_____

_____

_____

_____

Homophones

A. Use the homophone pairs in the box below to answer the questions.

fir/fur	to/two/too	fairy/ferry	tale/tail	meet/meat

1. Which word is an animal covering? _____

2. Which word is the rear part of an animal? _____

3. Which word is the part of a nut that you can eat? _____

4. Which word is the number that follows "one"? _____

5. Which word is a kind of boat? _____

B. Use the homophone pairs in the box in Part A to complete the sentences.

1. Hans Christian Andersen wrote many famous _____ tales.

2. Can you _____ me in the library this afternoon?

3. The soup is _____ hot to eat right now.

4. The forest was full of many tall _____ trees.

5. A tall _____ is a larger-than-life story.

C. Choose two homophone pairs from the box in Part A. Write a sentence using each word. Underline the homophone in each sentence.

1. Homophones: _____ and _____

   Sentence 1: _____

   _____

   Sentence 2: _____

   _____

2. Homophones: _____ and _____

   Sentence 1: _____

   _____

   Sentence 2: _____

   _____

Infinitives As Adjectives

A. Determine whether the infinitive in the sentence modifies the subject, the subject complement, the direct object, or the object of a preposition. Circle the correct answer.

1. This neighborhood will be one to watch this year.

   a. subject **b.** subject complement **c.** direct object **d.** object of a preposition

2. The first person to land on Mars may already have been born.

   a. subject **b.** subject complement **c.** direct object **d.** object of a preposition

3. I need someone to help me open this jar.

   a. subject **b.** subject complement **c.** direct object **d.** object of a preposition

4. Juanita searched for a way to enter.

   a. subject **b.** subject complement **c.** direct object **d.** object of a preposition

B. Fill in the blank with an infinitive that makes sense.

1. There is so much work _____ right now.

2. The problem _____ will be the drag on the car.

3. Nicole picked a song _____ at the talent show.

4. You keep asking about books _____ .

5. The spices _____ are cinnamon, cloves, and cardamom.

C. Choose one topic and write four sentences about it. Use at least four infinitives as adjectives. Possible topics:

a world record you'd like to break	what you think about 3D movies	the most important problem to solve in the world, in your opinion

1. _____

   _____

2. _____

   _____

3. _____

   _____

4. _____

   _____

Build Vocabulary

Critical Vocabulary

A. Read the sentences below. Circle the definition of each underlined word. Remember that you can look up any unfamiliar words in the dictionary.

1. You can find <u>contemporary</u> fiction in the front aisle of the bookstore. *Contemporary* means

   a. of the present time.   **b.** bestselling.   **c.** popular

2. The young hero finds himself trapped in a <u>dystopia</u>. A *dystopia* is

   a. a war novel.   **b.** a fictional unpleasant state.   **c.** a fictional heavenly state.

3. The heroes came finally face to face with their monstrous <u>adversary</u>. An *adversary* is

   a. an enemy.   **b.** a dragon.   **c.** a friend.

4. Young adult fiction is not <u>inferior</u> to adult fiction. *Inferior* means

   a. equal to.   **b.** greater in rank.   **c.** lower in rank.

B. Choose a word from the box to complete each sentence.

fiction	contemporary	dystopia	misfits
routine	supernatural	adversary	inferior

1. In this book, a group of _____ join a sports team and become more popular.

2. You can get into a reading _____ by picking up a book everyday.

3. _____ fiction can be very spooky.

4. _____ novels tell the stories of imaginary people and places.

5. Many books feature a hero and the hero's evil _____.

C. Choose three words from the box in Part B. Use each word in a sentence.

1. _____

_____

2. _____

_____

3. _____

_____

Academic Vocabulary

A. Choose the correct word from the box to complete each sentence and identify what part of speech it is in the sentence.

license	licensed

1. There is a debate about whether a sixteen-year-old should be able to get a driver's
   _____. Part of speech: _____

2. A _____ driver is much more likely to be safe on the roads than a driver without a
   license. Part of speech: _____

3. After four years of dental school, a student graduates as a _____ dentist.
   Part of speech: _____

4. Computer-chip makers _____ their technology to computer manufacturers.
   Part of speech: _____

B. Circle one of the choices and complete each sentence.

1. I (want/don't want) to get my driver's license as soon as possible because
   _____
   _____

2. I (think/don't think) bicyclists should have to be licensed because
   _____
   _____

C. Using one of the words from the box, write a sentence about whether you think people who text while driving should have their driver's licenses suspended.

   _____
   _____
   _____
   _____
   _____
   _____
   _____
   _____

Discuss the Purpose

Use the chart below to make notes about the genre descriptions you will be discussing.

Genre	Description	Notes

Analogies

A. Use the words from the box to complete each sentence.

genre	library	menu	meal
book	catalog	café	cuisine

1. A _____ is like a _____ because both are physical locations people can visit, and both offer a number of selections.

2. A _____ is like a _____ because both present a number of options in writing for individuals to choose from.

3. A _____ is like a _____ because both refer to a distinct style that appeals to a specific preference or taste.

4. A _____ is like a _____ because both describe individual items selected from a number of choices that can satisfy an individual's desire or appetite.

B. Use the words from the box below to complete the analogies. Each word will only be used once. Remember that analogies compare two things that have a purpose or one or more features in common.

genre	library	book	catalog

1. A _____ is like a flavor of ice cream.

2. A _____ is like a phone directory.

3. A _____ is like a television program.

4. A _____ is like a shopping mall.

C. Write your own analogies comparing a library, a genre, and a book to different nouns. For each analogy, write a sentence that explains the purpose or the feature(s) the two nouns have in common.

1. A library is like a _____.

   What do these two nouns have in common? _____

   _____

2. A book is like a _____.

   What do these two nouns have in common? _____

   _____

Write a Short Essay

My Favorite Genre

Introduction

What is your favorite genre?

_____

_____

_____

_____

Body

Why do you like this genre?

_____

_____

_____

_____

_____

What are some examples of this genre?

_____

_____

_____

_____

Conclusion

Summarize what you've said in a different way.

_____

_____

_____

_____

_____

Creating a Message

Write a radio advertisement for a book you loved. Write the way you would talk to a friend about something you're excited about. Keep the length of your ad to about one minute.

Introductory sentence Make it catchy.	

Body Briefly describe the book. Tell why you like it.	

Conclusion What do you want the listener to do?	

Latin Prefixes *Uni-* and *Super-*

A. Use the words in the box below to answer the questions.

supernatural	universe	superfluous	unilateral
superhuman	unicycle	superintendent	unify

1. Which word means "beyond the powers possessed by people"? _____

2. Which word means "to bring together into a single unit"? _____

3. Which word describes a device typically operated with pedals that has a single wheel? _____

4. Which word describes something that is beyond or more than what is needed? _____

5. Which word describes the sum of everything that exists? _____

B. Complete each sentence with a word from the box in Part A.
No word will be used more than once.

1. The leader's goal was to _____ all of the tiny states in the region into a single country.

2. His ability to lift cars and other massive objects was so incredible it seemed almost _____.

3. The boss made a _____ decision to introduce a dress code without asking any workers what they thought of the idea.

4. As the _____ of the school board, Ms. Walker is responsible for ensuring all students in the area have a positive learning environment.

5. The seven-hundred page novel was difficult to read because it contained so many _____ details about the characters and the setting.

6. Some of the most popular young adult novels in recent years have featured _____ beings like vampires and werewolves.

C. Choose three words from the table in Part A. Use each word in a sentence.
Underline the prefix *uni-* or *super-* in each word.

1. _____

_____

2. _____

_____

3. _____

_____

Critical Vocabulary

A. Read the sentences below. Circle the definition of each underlined word.
Remember that you can look up any unfamiliar words in the dictionary.

1. The population in my town grew from 300,000 people to over a million in the past decade.
   Population is

   a. a natural resource.

   b. the number of inhabitants of an area.

   c. the number of people who recycle.

2. Earth's resources, such as fossil fuels, water, and food, are limited. *Limited* means

   a. abundant.   **b.** restricted.   **c.** easily found.

3. I volunteered to distribute pamphlets about recycling at the school festival. *Distribute* means

   a. give something out.   **b.** cultivate.   **c.** save.

4. There are enough resources in the world for everyone to have enough to eat. *Resources* are

   a. a useful source of materials.   **b.** a rare source of materials.   **c.** renewable materials.

B. Choose a word from the box to complete each sentence.

population	replace	acknowledge	additional
limited	distribute	resources	reduce

1. We need to _____ the planet's problems.

2. There are some resources that we cannot _____ once gone.

3. We can easily _____ the amount of energy we use.

4. _____ plans on how to reduce energy and waste must be made.

5. The global _____ continues to keep growing.

C. Choose three words from the box in Part B. Use each word in a sentence.

1. _____

   _____

2. _____

   _____

3. _____

   _____

Adverbs

A. Determine whether the underlined adverb modifies a verb, an adjective, or another adverb.

1. The firewood burned <u>quickly</u>.

   a. verb   **b.** adjective   **c.** adverb

2. That trip was <u>more</u> tiring than I thought it would be.

   a. verb   **b.** adjective   **c.** adverb

3. Skye <u>usually</u> eats lunch around noon.

   a. verb   **b.** adjective   **c.** adverb

4. The train stopped <u>so</u> briefly that I couldn't get on.

   a. verb   **b.** adjective   **c.** adverb

B. Fill in the blank with an adverb that makes sense.

1. Could you speak more _____?

2. She _____ shook her head.

3. This shirt is_____ expensive than the other one.

4. The show aired _____ late for her to see it.

5. Fiona _____ reads for a while before going to sleep.

C. Choose one topic and write four sentences about it. Use adverbs to modify at least one adjective, at least one verb, and at least one other adverb. Possible topics:

something fun you can do without spending money	describe your greatest strength	what you would do with three wishes

1. _____

   _____

2. _____

   _____

3. _____

   _____

4. _____

   _____

Make Inferences

Make inferences based on lines 33–41 of the text "We Could Start Right Now."

Stated Directly	Inferences
"The average American uses four times as much electricity as the average inhabitant of Earth."	
"The average American uses over 300 liters of water each day, but 100 liters are sufficient for health and hygiene."	
"Electricity consumption includes the lights that are left on in empty rooms."	
"Water consumption includes waste from leaky pipes."	
"Food consumption includes food that is thrown away uneaten. (In fact, as much as 40% of the food produced in the U. S. goes to waste.)"	

What may happen if we do not monitor our use of resources? Cite evidence.

_____

_____

_____

_____

Academic Vocabulary

A. Read each sentence in the chart. Complete the chart by writing sufficient or insufficient.

Situation	Sufficient/Insufficient
A movie costs $6.5 million to make and takes in $10 million in ticket sales. The amount is…	
In his bibliography, Eric documented 30 of the 50 sources he used. The number of sources he documented was…	
The camp has 60 beds and 45 campers. The number of beds is…	
Anna got five hours of sleep last night. That amount of sleep is…	

B. Complete the answers with information from the text.

Mr. Brown had always wanted to have an island, so he bought one that is very small but sufficient for one simple house. He built a self-sufficient solar-powered house, and he is sufficiently fit to paddle to the island in a kayak. He can fish, but he has to bring in fruits and vegetables because the island has insufficient space for growing them.

1. What is the size of the island sufficient for?

The size is sufficient _____.

2. Why is Mr. Brown's house self-sufficient?

It's self-sufficient because it is _____.

3. Why is he able to paddle to the island in a kayak?

He's able to paddle to the island _____.

4. Why can't Mr. Brown grow crops on the island?

The island has _____.

C. Complete the sentences.

1. I am pretty self-sufficient because _____

_____.

2. If I had sufficient _____

_____.

Build Vocabulary

Critical Vocabulary

A. Circle the definition of each underlined word. Remember that you can look up any unfamiliar words in the dictionary.

1. As an orphan, I lived with my <u>cruel</u> aunt. *Cruel* means

    a. generous.   **b.** very mean.   **c.** elderly.

2. What <u>delusion</u> has come over me? A *delusion* is

    a. a belief that is not true.   **b.** a dream.   **c.** an illness.

3. I'll place a <u>wager</u> that the master admires her! A *wager* is

    a. a bet.   **b.** a halfhearted guess.   **c.** an idea.

4. I was surprised to see the same dog in the <u>parlor</u>. A *parlor* is

    a. a crate.   **b.** a sitting room.   **c.** a mansion.

B. Choose a word from the box to complete each sentence.

cruel	mercilessly	exposed	inherited	delusion	wager	parlor

1. The secret of the woman in the attic was soon _____ .

2. Jane had _____ a great deal of money.

3. Jane _____ confronted Mr. Rochester about keeping a secret from her.

4. Mr. Rochester thought he was having a _____ when Jane returned.

C. Choose three words from the box in Part B. Use each word in a sentence.

1. _____

    _____

    _____

2. _____

    _____

    _____

3. _____

    _____

    _____

USE WITH STUDENT BOOK pp. 167–173

The Vocabulary of Misfortune

All of the words in the box below are from the selection "Jane Eyre." They can all be considered part of the "vocabulary of misfortune."

A. Choose the correct words from the box below to answer each question.

blackened	bullied	cruel	epidemic	liar
mercilessly	orphan	ruin	terrible	vain

1. Which word describes a young person who does not have any parents? _____

2. Which word is a synonym for "mean" or "spiteful"? _____

3. Which word refers to an individual who does not tell the truth? _____

4. Which word can refer to a disease or illness affecting many individuals in an area? _____

5. Which word implies something was ineffective and did not produce the desired result? _____

B. Complete each sentence with the correct word from the box in Part A.
Each term will only be used once.

1. I stared at the _____ forest after the fire was put out and felt pity for the animals that had lost their homes.

2. I covered my eyes to block out the _____ sight of the monster on my television screen.

3. When children are _____ and teased at school, the best thing they can do is get help from a trusted adult.

4. The freezing rain _____ battered my exposed skin as I rushed home in the storm.

5. The ancient house was falling into _____ because it had been abandoned for so many years.

6. The best ways to protect yourself during a flu _____ are to wash your hands regularly and avoid coming into contact with people who are sick.

C. Choose four words from the box in Part A. Write a sentence using each term.
Underline the term in each sentence.

1. _____

2. _____

3. _____

4. _____

Build Vocabulary

Making Adjectives Into Nouns

A. Make each adjective in the table into a noun by adding the suffix *-ness*.

Adjective Form	Noun Form		Adjective Form	Noun Form
open			abrupt	
happy			pretty	
strange			calm	
friendly			routine	

B. Complete the sentences below using words from the table in Part A. For each sentence, decide whether the adjective form or the noun form of the word should be used.

1. He was usually quite a polite man, so his _____ when I spoke with him on the phone took me by surprise.

2. Because there was no wind, the surface of the lake was _____ and still.

3. It is easy to get lost in a _____ city if you don't have a map to help you find your way around.

4. Many people believe that the key to _____ is to remember to be grateful for everything you have.

5. I sat on the bench in my garden and took a few moments to admire the _____ of the many colorful flowers.

6. After several years of working at the same place and doing the same thing every day, the _____ of the job started to wear on me.

C. Choose two pairs of words from the table in Part A. Write one sentence using the adjective form of the word and one sentence using the noun form of the word. Underline the adjective forms and the noun forms in the sentences.

1: Word pair: _____ and _____

Sentence using adjective form: _____

_____

Sentence using noun form: _____

_____

2: Word pair: _____ and _____

Sentence using adjective form: _____

_____

Sentence using noun form: _____

_____

Infinitives As Adverbs

A. Determine which word in the sentence the infinitive modifies. Circle the correct answer.

1. Anthony waited impatiently to open the door.

   a. impatiently   **b.** waited   **c.** door   **d.** Anthony

2. Are you ready to leave yet?

   a. Are   **b.** you   **c.** ready   **d.** yet

3. I'm perfectly happy to stay out of the spotlight.

   a. perfectly   **b.** spotlight   **c.** out   **d.** happy

4. This meal is too much to eat all on my own.

   a. much   **b.** too   **c.** This   **d.** own

B. Fill in the blank with an infinitive that makes sense.

1. The actress came on stage _____ .

2. The puppy ran after the stick _____ it.

3. Ellen was delighted _____ that her class would be visiting the aquarium.

4. Simon went home early _____ from his cold.

5. I picked the green curtains _____ my tablecloth.

C. Choose one topic and write four sentences about it. Use at least two infinitives as adverbs. Possible topics:

something you would like to be famous for	a place you'd like to go on a class field trip	talk about the kind of day you are having today

1. _____

   _____

2. _____

   _____

3. _____

   _____

4. _____

   _____

Oral Reading

Be sure to use the Performance Task directions to fill out this chart, and assign roles to other students.

How many people will participate in the reading? *(If your group is large, you may want to divide the roles differently from the division in the Student Book.)*	
Will you stand up or sit down during the reading?	
Can everyone in the cast be heard at the back of the classroom?	
Will you have a rehearsal?	
Stage Manager	
Announcer	
Student A	
Student B	
Student C	

Social Class

Before answering the questions below, ask your teacher about England's class system and social structure in the 1840s. You can also find information online.

1. What social class is Edward Rochester? Why do you think so?

_____

_____

_____

_____

_____

_____

_____

2. What social class is Miss Ingram? Why do you think so?

_____

_____

_____

_____

_____

_____

_____

3. Is Jane Eyre the same social class as Mr. Rochester and Miss Ingram? Why do you think so?

_____

_____

_____

_____

_____

_____

_____

Build Vocabulary

Synonyms

A. Replace the words in parentheses with a synonym from the box.

revealed	pupil	assembled	fired	sweet	misty

1. The worker was (dismissed) _____ from his job after only a few weeks for frequently showing up late.

2. The teacher agreed to stay after school to help her (student) _____ complete a challenging assignment.

3. Almost everyone I know likes my best friend because she is such a (kindhearted) _____ person.

4. The driver turned on his headlights, but he still couldn't see very far because of the (foggy) _____ weather.

5. The newspaper article (exposed) _____ the company's lies and the approaches it used to intentionally mislead consumers.

6. A large group (gathered) _____ at the town hall to protest the closure of the community fitness center.

B. Write two synonyms for each word. You can use a dictionary or thesaurus to help you.

1. shocked _____ _____

2. gathered _____ _____

3. pupil _____ _____

4. dismissed _____ _____

C. Choose two synonym pairs from Part B. Use each synonym in a sentence. Underline the synonyms.

Synonyms: _____ and _____

Sentence 1: _____

Sentence 2: _____

Synonyms: _____ and _____

Sentence 1: _____

Sentence 2: _____

Performance Task

Narrative Presentation Story Ideas

A. Here is a list of the reading and podcast selections in this unit. Pick three of the selections and describe the main idea of each one you choose.

"Placido's Place"   "The Young Adults Café"

"The Quinceañera Text"   "We Could Start Right Now"

"Before They Were Presidents"   "Jane Eyre"

"Podcast: The Fir Tree"

_____

_____

_____

_____

_____

_____

B. Write three possible main ideas for your story.

Idea 1

_____

_____

_____

Idea 2

_____

_____

_____

Idea 3

_____

_____

_____

_____

Plan your Narrative Presentation

To evaluate your narrative presentation, use the Narrative Oral Presentation Rubric available from your online Student Resources or from your teacher.

Story Idea

Write your story idea. Remember, you can write either in the first or third person.

_____

_____

Characters

The main character is _____.

Other characters are _____.

Describe what makes the characters believable. _____

_____

Describe what the main character looks like. _____

_____

Describe the relationships between characters. _____

_____

Setting

How does the setting contribute to the story? [Hint: Setting includes more than just place and time. It also includes cultural influences such as dress, speech, and customs.] _____

_____

What are some precise words you can use to describe the setting? _____

_____

Conflict or Problem

What is the problem or struggle that the characters face? _____

_____

Language

What connecting and time-order words will you use? _____

_____

Academic Vocabulary

A. Read the paragraph. Complete the answers with information from the text.

> There is a trend toward healthier eating in the United States. The menus at trendy restaurants contain more vegetable dishes. Actors and other trendsetters are becoming vegetarians and vegans. The latest trend is raw food restaurants.

1. Is there a trend toward fried food or healthy eating in the U.S.?

There is a trend _____.

2. What kinds of restaurants have vegetable dishes on their menus?

_____ have more vegetable dishes.

3. Who are becoming vegetarians and vegans?

_____ are becoming vegetarians and vegans.

4. What is the latest trend in restaurants?

The latest trend is _____.

B. Complete the sentence starters.

1. If I were a trendsetter, I would _____.

2. I have noticed a trend toward _____.

C. Using at least one word from the box, write two sentences about a trend you like, explaining why you think this has become popular.

trend	trendy	trendsetter

1. _____

_____

_____

2. _____

_____

_____

Finalize Your Plan

WRITING TOOLBOX

Elements of a Narrative

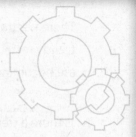

Climax

Rising Action

Falling Action

Resolution

Exposition

▸ **Exposition** — The exposition is the introduction to the narrative. It's the part of the story where you will present the main character, setting, and conflict.

▸ **Rising Action** — This is where you will describe the obstacles that the character must overcome. You'll start to build suspense and lay out the direction the narrative is heading.

▸ **Climax** — This part of your narrative is the most important or exciting event. It's where your story "comes to a boil"— something happens that can't be ignored, and things change rapidly.

▸ **Falling Action** — The falling action describes how the conflict is resolved, and reveals the moral lesson—if there is one—that the character learns.

▸ **Resolution** — This is the final part of the plot, where you tie up any loose ends and answer any questions that remain.

A. Review the elements of a narrative story above. Describe the elements in your short story.

Exposition _____

_____

Rising Action _____

_____

Climax _____

_____

Falling Action _____

_____

Resolution _____

_____

B. Write a brief summary of your narrative.

_____

_____

Vocabulary Review

Here are some of the words you learned in this unit. Choose words from this list and sort them into the categories below. There are many possible correct answers! Also, many of the words fit into more than one category.

abruptness	cruel	gratitude	misty	sufficient
adore	debate	happiness	openness	superfluous
book	deduce	hare	optimist	supernatural
bullied	dystopia	honey	parlor	terrible
broom	epidemic	insufficient	plunder	trend
catalogue	friendliness	library	privilege	type
clear	genre	license	ruin	universe
contemporary	gilded	mercilessly	strangeness	vain

Nouns

1. _____
2. _____
3. _____
4. _____

Adjectives

1. _____
2. _____
3. _____
4. _____

Words with Suffixes

1. _____
2. _____
3. _____
4. _____

Multiple-Meaning Words

1. Word: _____

   Definition 1: _____

   Definition 2: _____

2. Word: _____

   Definition 1: _____

   Definition 2: _____

Easily Confused Words

A. **Circle the correct word in each sentence. Use the context clues to help you decide.**

1. You have my [empathy, sympathy] for your loss.

2. I have [ambiguous, ambivalent] feelings on whether students should wear uniforms.

3. Please [accept, except] this small token of our appreciation.

4. If it's cold outside, I usually [wear, where] a sweater.

B. **Fill in the blanks with the correct word that fits in the context of the sentence.**

1. Sarah likes all kinds of chocolate _____ white chocolate.

2. I try to have _____ for the villains in the story and understand why they act the way they do.

3. These guidelines are _____ on the question of how to record the data.

4. _____ do you think you're going with that?

5. I won't _____ anything less than the best.

C. **Write four sentences, one using *empathy* or *sympathy*, one using *ambiguous* or *ambivalent*, one using *accept* or *except*, and one using *wear* or *where*. Your sentences should demonstrate your understanding of the meaning of each word.**

1. _____

_____

_____

2. _____

_____

_____

3. _____

_____

_____

4. _____

_____

_____

Personal Legacy

"Our memory is a more perfect world than the universe: it gives back life to those who no longer exist."

—Guy de Maupassant, writer

What do you think of when you hear the word "legacy"? Make visual or written notes.

What is an important legacy that someone has given you?

_____
_____
_____
_____

What was Thomas Jefferson's personal legacy?

_____
_____
_____
_____

How would you like people to remember you? What will you have to do to accomplish this?

_____
_____
_____
_____

Academic Vocabulary

As you work through Unit 5 look and listen for these words. Practice using them when you talk in class and in your writing. Write about your experiences using these words in the last column of the chart.

Word	Definition	Related Forms	My Experiences
communicate	to give information or exchange ideas	communication, communicator, communicative	
draft	• to write early versions of a document • early versions of a written document		
liberation	the act of freeing or the state of being free	liberate, liberator	
philosophy	• a set of beliefs about life that guide a person's behavior • the study of the nature and meaning of life	philosopher, philosophical	
publish	• to prepare and produce a book or other material for people to read • to produce and share written material	publishing, publisher, publication, public	

Shakespeare's Legacy of Words

Complete the chart with the word origin and a sample sentence in which the word is used. Write *n*, *adj*, *v*, and so on for each word part. If necessary, look up the word origin or etymology of the word in a dictionary or online etymology website. The first one has been done for you.

Word	Word Parts/Origin (optional)	Sentence
cold-hearted (adj.)	cold (adj) + heart (n) + ed (suffix)	We knew he was coldhearted when he ignored the puppy's whining.
fashionable (adj.)		
gloomy (adj.)		
hurry (v.)		
lonely (adj.)		
moonbeam (n.)		
zany (adj.)		

Invent a Word

Invent a word that defines your legacy. Imagine it is 100 years from now. What would you like your legacy to be? Make up a word that describes how you would like to be remembered. Use the questions below to help you.

1. What are some qualities you would like people to remember about you?
You can use more than one word to describe each quality.

_____

_____

_____

2. Imagine you are 65 years older than you are now, looking back at your life.
What are some things you've done that you'd like people to remember?

_____

_____

_____

3. List at least five words or phrases that relate to the way you'd like to be remembered.
These are real words, not words you make up.

_____

_____

_____

4. Use the dictionary or a thesaurus to find synonyms for the words you wrote for item 3.

_____

_____

_____

5. Pick three words or terms that you think best describe you or your legacy. Combine words, add suffixes or prefixes to make new words, or change the words in any way to make new words. Let your imagination go. Write everything down without censoring anything. Then go back and choose the new word or term you like best.

_____

_____

_____

_____

_____

_____

Critical Vocabulary

A. Read these sentences from the selection. Circle the definition of each underlined word. Remember that you can look up any unfamiliar words in the dictionary.

1. You know my policy about not naming people on the blog unless they are already famous. A *policy* is

    a. a rule.   **b.** a goal.   **c.** a dream.

2. For a while, I thought about what personal achievements I should put in the box. *Achievements* are

    a. tasks done successfully.   **b.** fun memories.   **c.** records.

3. I began by itemizing what other people thought of me. *Itemizing* means

    a. remembering.   **b.** listing.   **c.** asking.

4. My family wouldn't fit in a box, even if I could persuade them it was for a good cause. To *persuade* means

    a. to ask kindly.   **b.** to remember.   **c.** to convince.

B. Choose a word from the box to complete each sentence.

policy	fascinating	itemizing	accomplishment	persuade

1. Graduating with honors is a big _____ for students.

2. I started by _____ the items I'd like to put in a time capsule.

3. Maybe I can _____ you to write an article on my blog sometime.

4. Mr. X gave us a _____ assignment last week that really captured my interest.

5. The school _____ does not allow students to use cell phones in class.

C. Choose three words from the box in Part B. Use each word in a sentence.

1. _____

_____

_____

2. _____

_____

_____

3. _____

_____

_____

Prepositional Phrases

A. Decide if the <u>underlined preposition</u> in the sentence is modifying the subject, direct object, or subject complement. Circle the correct answer.

1. Theo found the letter <u>between</u> the couch and the wall.

    a. subject   **b.** direct object   **c.** subject complement   **d.** none of the above

2. Mr. Vasquez was the police chief <u>of</u> Laketown.

    a. subject   **b.** direct object   **c.** subject complement   **d.** none of the above

3. The kid <u>under</u> the blanket reads in bed.

    a. subject   **b.** direct object   **c.** subject complement   **d.** none of the above

4. Yi-Jun is the wrestler <u>with</u> the thickest neck.

    a. subject   **b.** direct object   **c.** subject complement   **d.** none of the above

B. Fill in the blank with a preposition that fits.

1. Aww, the dog _____ the table is snoring.

2. Uncle's diploma is _____ the desk in his office.

3. Traffic is delayed _____ 14th Street.

4. Rasheed _____ the street runs laps at the gym.

5. Mimi found a box _____ spare parts.

C. Choose one topic and write four sentences about it. Use at least four prepositions in the paragraph as adjectives. Possible topics:

finding something mysterious in a house	giving directions to someone who's lost	where someone came from and where they are now

1. _____

    _____

2. _____

    _____

3. _____

    _____

4. _____

    _____

Collaborative Discussion Support

Read the assignment on Student Book page 186.

Part A: Discussing the Purpose

1. What were some of Janet's interests that she wanted to symbolize?

_____

_____

_____

2. What objects did Janet choose to represent her interests?

_____

_____

_____

3. How did the objects Janet chose represent the things she said she cared about?

_____

_____

_____

_____

4. What do the objects Janet chose tell you about her as a person? Why?

_____

_____

_____

Part B: Making Predictions

5. What interests does Janet mention in the text for which she had no matching object?

_____

_____

_____

6. What might Janet have put into the box that she doesn't mention? Think of her interests and her personality.

_____

_____

_____

Shades of Meaning: Connotation

A word's connotation is the set of ideas and feelings associated with the word, as opposed to its dictionary definition. Connotations can be positive or negative.

1	people	community	mob
2	mentor	disciplinarian	teacher
3	fat	colossal	big
4	interested	obsessed	fascinated
5	bother	show concern	pressure

A. Choose the correct answer from the words in the box.

1. In row 2 which word has a negative connotation? _____

2. In row 2 which word has a very positive connotation of someone who guides and inspires? _____

3. In row 5 which word has a negative connotation? _____

4. In row 1 which word has a negative connotation for a group of people? _____

B. Complete the sentence with the correct word from the box.

1. Whenever an accident or tragedy occurs the _____ comes together to offer help and support.

2. Our solar system is so _____ that scientists to this day have not yet discovered it completely.

3. Kim was _____ in understanding how magnetism works.

4. The _____ became angry and quickly was out of control.

C. Choose three words from the box. Use each word in a sentence that shows its connotative meaning.

1. _____

_____

2. _____

_____

3. _____

_____

Decide What to Write

Answer the questions to help you decide what to write in your comment.

1. Review the second paragraph of Janet's blog where she describes the assignment.

   What did you like about the assignment? Why? _____

   _____

   _____

   Describe anything you didn't like about the assignment. _____

   _____

   _____

2. What are one or two of your interests? _____

   _____

   _____

   _____

3. What objects might you use to symbolize your interests? _____

   _____

   _____

   _____

   Write any other ideas you have for your comment. _____

   _____

   _____

   _____

   _____

   _____

   _____

   _____

Academic Vocabulary

To evaluate your blog, use the Blog Rubric available from your online Student Resources or from your teacher.

Use the questions to help you design and write your blog.

1. What do I want my blog to do: Inform? Educate? Entertain? Some combination?

_____

_____

_____

_____

2. What voice will I use? How can I write my blog as if I'm talking to the reader in person? Is this my first blog, or do I already have a community of followers? How will that affect the way I start my blog?

_____

_____

_____

_____

3. What am I going to write about? What details do I want to give people?

_____

_____

_____

_____

4. How will I start my blog post? (Think of a sentence that will catch your reader's interest!)

_____

_____

_____

_____

5. What software will I use to write my blog? Will I host my blog on my own website or use one of the online blogging hosts?

_____

_____

_____

_____

Build Vocabulary

Academic Vocabulary

A. Complete each sentence with the correct word from the box.

communicate	communication

1. My friend doesn't use his email often; he prefers face-to-face _____.

communicator	communicates

2. If you run for office, you need to have good ideas but you also need to be a good _____.

communicate	communicative

3. Melinda is very _____ on her opinions about popular music.

communicative	communicates

4. The writer _____ her point of view through her word choices.

B. Read the passage and answer the questions.

> Some teenagers seem to prefer digital communication when talking with their friends.
> They consider people who know all the texting slang to be great communicators.
> They are very communicative because they send texts every few minutes.

1. What do some teenagers seem to prefer?

Some teenagers _____.

2. Who do they consider to be the great communicators?

They consider people _____.

3. How are they communicative?

They are communicative _____.

communicate	communication

C. Using a word from the box, write a sentence or two telling what your favorite method of communication is and why you like it.

_____

_____

_____

Information

Answer the questions about *Time Capsule*.

1. Who is the team?

   _____

2. What did each kid have to select for the time capsule?

   _____

   _____

3. What did the kids do first to prepare?

   _____

   _____

4. What does Amalia choose as her objects?

   _____

   _____

5. What does Zane choose as his objects?

   _____

   _____

6. What does Malik choose as his objects?

   _____

   _____

Compare and Contrast

Think about the video you have just seen. Compare and contrast it with "Janet's Planet."

1. What common topic do the video and the blog share?

   _____

2. What difference do you see between the video and the blog?

   _____

   _____

3. What objects would you include in your time capsule? Explain.

   _____

   _____

   _____

Build Vocabulary

Critical Vocabulary

A. Circle four words in the Word Bank that you want to know more about.

> ### Word Bank
>
> | | | | | | |
> |---|---|---|---|---|---|
> | contribute | statement | concept | lullaby's | represents | events |
> | remind | liberating | pursue | elected | capsule | |

B. Watch the video *Time Capsule* again and listen for the words. Complete the activity.

1. Word: _____

What I think it means: _____

What it means: _____

2. Word: _____

What I think it means: _____

What it means: _____

3. Word: _____

What I think it means: _____

What it means: _____

4. Word: _____

What I think it means: _____

What it means: _____

C. Choose three words that you wrote in Part B. Write a sentence using each word.

1. _____

_____

_____

2. _____

_____

_____

3. _____

_____

Critical Vocabulary

A. Read the sentences below. Circle the definition of each underlined word. Remember that you can look up any unfamiliar words in the dictionary.

1. The party is an <u>exclusive</u> affair. *Exclusive* means

    a. open.   **b.** limited to a certain group.   **c.** entertaining.

2. The musical spoofs poked fun at the <u>foibles</u> of the justices. *Foibles* are

    a. minor weaknesses.   **b.** voices.   **c.** major political mistakes.

3. He mentioned the <u>customary</u> platters that would be offered at the party. *Customary* means

    a. according to usual practices.   **b.** unique.   **c.** fancy.

4. Sotomayor challenges <u>boundaries</u> and disrupts the norm. *Boundaries* are

    a. limits.   **b.** lawsuits.   **c.** prejudices.

B. Choose a word from the box to complete each sentence.

exclusive	customary	parodies	reveled
foibles	decorum	permeated	boundaries

1. When attending such a fancy party, we must be sure to follow the proper _____.

2. You can guarantee that only an _____ group of politicians will be invited to the private event.

3. Certain stuffy attitudes and behaviors had _____ the party.

4. The members of the Supreme Court are familiar with each other's quirks and _____.

5. Sotomayor _____ in the attention after throwing the first pitch at a Yankee game.

C. Choose three words from the box in Part B. Use each word in a sentence.

1. _____

   _____

2. _____

   _____

3. _____

   _____

Multiple-Meaning Words

A. Choose the response that correctly defines the underlined word.

1. Marlene and her friends were very much looking forward to the <u>social</u> on Thursday night.

   a. an informal event for members of a group   **b.** liking to be with and talking to people

2. Raul Martinez is serving his third <u>term</u> in the U.S. Senate.

   a. a specified amount of time   **b.** a word or phrase that has an exact meaning

3. My four-year-old niece just loves to <u>skip</u>.

   a. pass over or omit   **b.** move forward with leaps and bounds

4. The <u>bear</u> looked as if it was about to attack.

   a. to carry   **b.** large, heavy animal with thick hair and sharp claws

5. Try to <u>place</u> your keys in the same spot so that you can always find them.

   a. put   **b.** a specific area

B. Define each underlined word.

1. The loss of his father was more than the young man could <u>bear</u>.

   _____

2. Ed decided to <u>skip</u> the third question on the test.

   _____

3. Megan loves to be with friends; she is a very <u>social</u> person.

   _____

4. He threw the <u>pitch</u> fast but right up the middle of home plate.

   _____

5. Let's picnic at the same <u>place</u> we went to last week.

   _____

bear	place	social	pitch	term	skip

C. Choose two words from the box. Use each word in two sentences that show different meanings of the word.

1. _____

   _____

2. _____

   _____

Participle Phrases

A. Decide if the underlined participle is modifying a subject or a direct object.

1. The damaged vase is right here.

   a. subject   **b.** direct object

2. Joan found the chirping bird in a tall tree.

   a. subject   **b.** direct object

3. The boat followed the rushing currents.

   a. subject   **b.** direct object

4. The sleeping bear opened one eye.

   a. subject   **b.** direct object

B. Fill in the blank with a participle that fits.

1. The _____ machine should be easy to fix.

2. The _____ machine doesn't need to be fixed.

3. Emma found a _____ bird.

4. Jane found the book _____ to read.

5. Hector completed the _____ race.

C. Choose one topic and write four sentences about it. Use at least three participles in the paragraph. Possible topics:

how someone feels about another person	a way of getting somewhere	animals doing cute things

1. _____

   _____

2. _____

   _____

3. _____

   _____

4. _____

   _____

Supporting Details

Write text evidence that the author used to support the following observations. Reread pages 189–194 in the Student Book and answer the questions below.

1. what the party is usually like

_____

_____

_____

_____

_____

_____

2. Sotomayor's actions before the party

_____

_____

_____

_____

_____

_____

3. how the justices reacted to Sotomayor's invitations to dance

_____

_____

_____

_____

_____

4. how Ginsburg reacted to dancing with Sotomayor

_____

_____

_____

_____

_____

_____

Sonia Sotomayor

Find reliable sources of information about Sonia Sotomayor. You can look for information about any part of her life. Complete the worksheet showing one or more examples from each kind of source.

Online informational source: _____

_____

Why it is a reliable source: _____

_____

_____

_____

_____

Print source: _____

_____

Why it is a reliable source: _____

_____

_____

_____

_____

Other media source: _____

_____

Why it is a reliable source: _____

_____

_____

_____

_____

Build Vocabulary

Academic Vocabulary

A. Are these tasks related to writing a first draft or final draft? Circle the appropriate answer.

1. Brainstorm ideas   FIRST DRAFT   FINAL DRAFT

2. Incorporate feedback   FIRST DRAFT   FINAL DRAFT

3. Think of a strong opening sentence   FIRST DRAFT   FINAL DRAFT

4. Add edits from your proofreading partner   FIRST DRAFT   FINAL DRAFT

5. Format the draft for submission   FIRST DRAFT   FINAL DRAFT

B. Complete the answers with information from the text.

> Diplomats from many countries met to begin drafting an international agreement about environmental sustainability. They knew that it would be difficult to get all the countries to approve the agreement and that they would have to write many drafts before they finished.

1. What did the diplomats meet to do?

The diplomats met to _____ .

2. Why did they think they would have to write many drafts?

They would have to write many drafts because it _____

_____ .

C. Using a form of *draft*, write a sentence about the difference between the first draft of a report and the finished report.

_____

_____

_____

_____

_____

_____

_____

_____

Deconstructing a Sentence

Identify each part of this sentence from the selection.

> Her close friend Justice Antonin Scalia, always an easy target in the law clerks' parodies because of his exaggerated mannerisms, secured a spot along a back wall of the room.

Subject: _____

Verb: _____

Object: _____

Phrases that modify the subject: _____

_____

_____

_____

_____

_____

Phrases that modify the object: _____

_____

_____

_____

_____

Examine Text Structure For Genre

Part A:

Describe the text features that explain the genre of each selection.

"Janet's Planet"—personal narrative: _____

_____

_____

"Life of the Party"—narrative nonfiction: _____

_____

_____

Part B:

Use the features to identify the genre and type for each of the following:

1. Toast two slices of bread.

   Spread one piece of toast with peanut butter.

   Spread the other piece of toast with jelly.

   Make a sandwich with the two pieces of toast.

   Genre and type: _____

2. Instead of swimming through a school of colorful fish, Anna kept seeing strange swirling colors. Disgusted, she pulled off the headset, made a few adjustments, and placed it back over her head. The flickering pinpoints of light were almost painful. She blinked. But the next thing she saw made her blood run cold. Alien symbols streamed across the screen, followed by a face like none she had ever seen . . . or imagined.

   Genre: _____

3. McKenzie was a person who

   could put both feet into one shoe.

   This fit in with his cunning plans

   to wear the other on his hands.

   Genre: _____

Idioms

kick up your heels		barrel ahead
	for better or for worse	
down-to-the-minute		two left feet

A. Choose the correct word from the box to answer each question.

1. Which idiom means "go straight ahead, at a high rate of speed, toward a goal"? _____

2. Which idiom describes someone who moves in an awkward way when dancing? _____

3. Which idiom means "happens whether the results are good or bad"? _____

4. Which idiom means "doing things that you enjoy"? _____

B. Complete each sentence with a phrase from the box.

1. We did our best to prepare, so _____ we'll give our presentation tomorrow.

2. Manny had what he thought was a great idea and so decided to just _____ with it, no matter what other people thought.

3. Your graduation party might be a good time to _____.

4. No matter how hard he tries, Charlie dances with _____.

C. Choose three idioms from the box. Use each idiom in a sentence.

1. _____

_____

2. _____

_____

3. _____

_____

Podcast: "'Satchmo'—The Father of Jazz"

Setting a Purpose

Read pages 196 and 197 of the Student Book to complete this page.

How did Armstrong influence the world as a musician?	How did Armstrong inspire others as an individual?

Build Vocabulary

Critical Vocabulary

A. Circle the definition of each underlined word. Remember that you can look up any unfamiliar words in the dictionary.

1. From an early age, he was a musical <u>prodigy</u>—music came naturally to him. A *prodigy* is

   a. a student.   **b.** a young person with exceptional talent.   **c.** a teacher.

2. African American musicians criticized him for being out of touch and <u>complacent</u>. *Complacent* means

   a. self-satisfied.   **b.** angry.   **c.** forgetful.

3. Armstrong's popularity <u>transcended</u> racial barriers. *Trancended* means

   a. to go beyond.   **b.** to agree with.   **c.** to ignore.

4. He drafted hundreds of letters and <u>memoir</u> pages in his life. A *memoir* is

   a. an article.   **b.** a biography.   **c.** a photoessay.

B. Choose a word from the box to complete each sentence.

prodigy	legacy	transcended	innate
complacent	memoir	beaming	scat

1. Satchmo always had a _____ grin on his face while performing on stage.
2. _____ singing changed jazz music.
3. The _____ of jazz music lives on in popular music.
4. Musicians can learn a lot from reading Satchmo's personal _____ .
5. Scat singers have an _____ talent for rhthym and melody.

C. Choose three words from the box in Part B. Use each word in a sentence.

1. _____

   _____

2. _____

   _____

3. _____

   _____

USE WITH STUDENT BOOK pp. 196–197, AND THE
PODCAST "'SATCHMO'—THE FATHER OF JAZZ"

Collaborative Discussion Support

As you listen to the podcast, focus on the answers to these questions.

Question:	Answers:
What personal qualities contributed to Louis Armstrong's success?	_____ _____ _____ _____ _____ _____ _____ _____ _____
In what ways did Armstrong influence the world?	_____ _____ _____ _____ _____ _____ _____ _____ _____
What parts of Armstrong's legacy still resound today?	_____ _____ _____ _____ _____ _____ _____ _____ _____

Homophones

A. **Circle the correct homophone.**

1. Which word means "in this place"?

   a. here   **b.** hear

2. Which word means "to have information in your mind"?

   a. no   **b.** know

3. Which word means "a view or sight that looks like a picture"?

   a. scene   **b.** seen

4. Which word means "a woman thought to have magical powers"?

   a. witch   **b.** which

5. Which word means "a box used for storing things"?

   a. been   **b.** bin

B. **Complete each sentence with the correct homophone.**

1. Berto has _____ playing basketball for two hours. (been, bin)

2. That is certainly a large _____ of money! (some, sum)

3. The character I play doesn't say anything until the second _____. [seen, scene]

4. _____ of us are going to the concert tomorrow night. (Some, Sum)

5. In the play, the _____ is an evil woman. (witch, which)

C. **Choose two homophone sets from the box. Use each word in a sentence.**

no/know	hear/here	been/bin	seen/scene	some/sum	which/witch

1. _____

   _____

   _____

2. _____

   _____

   _____

Gerunds

A. Decide if the underlined <u>gerund</u> is a subject or an object. Circle the correct answer.

1. <u>Running</u> up the hill was tough.

    a. subject   **b.** object

2. We found the mouse <u>hiding</u> under the couch.

    a. subject   **b.** object

3. <u>Biking</u> is a lot of fun.

    a. subject   **b.** object

4. A quick repair stopped the door's <u>squeaking</u>.

    a. subject   **b.** object

B. Fill in the blank with a gerund that fits.

1. _____ is good exercise.

2. _____ is a bad idea.

3. The doctor told me that _____ too much is dangerous.

4. Mr. Gallopp doesn't like _____ on uncomfortable chairs.

5. Kvehl enjoys _____ at the beach.

C. Choose one topic and write four sentences about it. Use at least three gerunds.
Possible topics:

exercising	relaxing	working

1. _____

_____

2. _____

_____

3. _____

_____

4. _____

_____

Greek and Latin Roots

uniform	solo	innate	legacy	autobiography

A. Choose a word from the box to answer each question.

1. Which word means "inborn, natural"? _____

2. Which word means "a type of clothing worn by people belonging to the same group or organization"? _____

3. Which word means "something transmitted or received from an ancestor"? _____

4. Which word means "the story of a person's life written by that person"? _____

5. Which word means "a piece of music performed or sung by a single person"? _____

B. Complete each sentence with a word from the box.

1. Frank's _____ distrust of authority figures frequently got him into trouble.

2. The athlete's _____ to the entire sports world was his tremendous sense of fair play.

3. Bettina was confident that her concert _____ would go well.

4. The waiters all wore the same _____ .

5. I read the writer's _____ and thoroughly enjoyed it.

C. Choose four words from the box. Use each word in a sentence.

1. _____

_____

2. _____

_____

3. _____

_____

4. _____

_____

Academic Vocabulary

A. Complete each sentence with the correct word from the box.

liberate	liberation	liberator

1. Gandhi worked to _____ India from British rule.
2. People who are not free dream of _____ .
3. Many countries have had _____ movements.
4. Simón Bolívar is known as a _____ in South America's struggle for independence from Spain.

B. Complete each sentence.

1. If I had super powers, I would liberate _____
_____
_____ .

2. We could call Abraham Lincoln a liberator because he _____
_____
_____ .

C. The inventors of the Internet thought it would be a tool of liberation that could make people's lives more convenient. Using a word from the box, write a sentence explaining what the Internet would liberate people from.

_____
_____
_____
_____
_____
_____
_____
_____

Critical Vocabulary

A. **Read the sentences below. Circle the definition of each underlined word. Remember that you can look up any unfamiliar words in the dictionary.**

1. The U.S. president <u>appoints</u> the justices. *Appoints* means

   a. fires.   **b.** assigns.   **c.** appeals to.

2. The decision said <u>segregation</u> was allowed as long as there were "separate but equal" facilities for the races. *Segregation* means

   a. enforced togetherness.   **b.** enforced separation.   **c.** enforced rules.

3. The unanimous *Loving v. Virginia* decision in 1967 struck down a law <u>prohibiting</u> interracial marriage. *Prohibiting* means

   a. allowing.   **b.** forbidding.   **c.** engaging.

4. Clarence Earl Gideon was <u>convicted</u> of breaking into a pool hall and stealing a few dollars in coins. *Convicted* means

   a. suspected of being guilty.   **b.** found innocent.   **c.** declared guilty.

B. **Choose a word from the box to complete each sentence.**

appoints	appealed	majority	dissents
segregation	prohibiting	convicted	testimony

1. The lawyer tried to poke holes in the witness's _____ .

2. The justices's _____ thoroughly explained why they thought the decision of the majority was wrong.

3. If a _____ of justices vote against a decision, then that decision will not be put into effect.

4. The man was _____ of being guilty after the jury heard the evidence and made its decision.

C. **Choose three words from the box in Part B. Use each word in a sentence.**

1. _____

   _____

2. _____

   _____

3. _____

   _____

Collaborative Discussion Support

As you reread the selection, focus on the answers to these questions.

1. What is the primary role of Supreme Court justices?

_____

_____

2. How do the justices decide cases? Why do they sometimes have to interpret the Constitution?

_____

_____

_____

_____

3. What are the main ideas in each section?

The Court in Brief: _____

_____

The Final Word: _____

_____

Guided by the Constitution: _____

_____

_____

Overturning Laws: _____

_____

_____

Opinions and Dissents: _____

_____

_____

Constitutional Amendments: _____

_____

Reconsidering Decisions: _____

_____

_____

A Petition in Pencil: _____

_____

_____

_____

Specialized Vocabulary

| hearing | cases | rulings | precedents | arguments | opinions | dissents |

A. Choose the correct word from the box to answer each question.

1. Which word means "judicial decisions that serve as an authority for deciding later cases"?
_____

2. Which word means "coherent sets of reasons that support a particular point of view on a case"?
_____

3. Which word means "decisions made by a judge or judges"? _____

4. Which word means "actions or lawsuits that are tried in a court of law"? _____

5. Which word means "disagreements by one or more judges with the decision of the majority"?
_____

B. Read the passage. Then complete the sentences about the passage.

The hearing in the Court of Appeals was scheduled for March 31st. The case was argued before seven judges. The lawyer for the defense gave very convincing arguments that her client was innocent. The opposing lawyer cited legal precedents to prove her case.

The majority of the judges agreed that the defendant won the cases, but two judges wrote dissents that they did not agree.

1. The _____ was scheduled for March 31st.

2. The lawyer for the defense gave very convincing _____ .

3. The opposing lawyer cited legal _____ to prove her case.

4. Both judges wrote their _____ concerning the majority opinion of the Court.

C. Choose three words from the box. Use each word in a sentence.

1. _____
_____

2. _____
_____

3. _____
_____

Write On! Support

Read the Write On! section of Student Book p. 203 to complete this page.

Supreme Court Justices are appointed for life.	
Advantages	_____ _____ _____ _____ _____ _____ _____ _____ _____ _____ _____ _____
Disadvantages	_____ _____ _____ _____ _____ _____ _____ _____ _____ _____ _____ _____

The Prefixes *un*– and *pre*–

uncomfortable	unlike	unconstitutional	unable
prejudge	preview	prefabricate	prepaid

A. Choose a word from the box to answer each question.

1. Which word means "an advance viewing or exhibition"? _____ .

2. Which word means "different from"? _____

3. Which word means "a feeling of unease"? _____

4. Which word means "to put parts together at a factory so that construction consists mainly of reassembling the parts"? _____

5. Which word means "to judge beforehand without possessing adequate knowledge"? _____ .

B. Complete each sentence with a word from the box.

1. The postage on the envelope was _____ .

2. The opposition argued that the lower court's decision was _____ .

3. Marco's constant teasing made Bettina _____ .

4. We saw a _____ of a film before it was released for the general public.

5. No matter how hard she tried, Latoya was _____ to swim the length of the pool.

C. Choose three words from the box. Use each word in a sentence.

1. _____
   _____

2. _____
   _____

3. _____
   _____

Infinitive Phrases

A. Decide which noun the underlined infinitive modifies and whether that noun is a subject or a direct object. Circle the correct answer.

1. The contest <u>to be</u> the top juggler happens today.

   a. contest, subject **b.** contest, direct object **c.** today, subject **d.** today, direct object

2. Mrs. Williams postponed the essay <u>to write</u> for Friday.

   a. Mrs. Williams, subject **b.** Mrs. Williams, direct object **c.** essay, subject **d.** essay, direct object

3. Ellie enjoyed the chance <u>to show</u> off her skills.

   a. Ellie, subject **b.** Ellie, direct object **c.** chance, subject **d.** chance, direct object

4. That jump <u>to catch</u> the ball impressed everyone.

   a. jump, subject **b.** jump, direct object **c.** ball, subject **d.** ball, direct object

B. Fill in the blank with <u>an infinitive</u> that fits.

1. Mauro and Liz both want _____ the best at this game.

2. Her mom gave her gloves _____ her stay warm.

3. I asked Carlos _____ the computer.

4. The team was able _____ an answer.

5. Are you ready _____ a new book?

C. Choose one topic and write at least four sentences about it. The paragraph must include at least three infinitives. Possible topics:

reasons to play your favorite game	a contest to get a prize	ways to have fun

1. _____

   _____

2. _____

   _____

3. _____

   _____

4. _____

   _____

Academic Vocabulary

A. Complete each sentence with the correct word from the box.

philosophical philosophers

1. Many _____ have their own theories about the meaning of life.

philosophy philosophical

2. The president says he doesn't have a _____ objection to the idea.

philosophy philosophical

3. When I meet new people, my _____ is to believe that they are nice unless they show me that they're not.

philosopher philosophy

4. The *Yi Jing*, a book of Chinese _____, was first published around 672 BCE.

B. Complete each sentence.

1. Philosophers think about what happiness is; I think happiness is _____
_____.

2. Aristotle said that friendship is a partnership; my philosophy about friendship is _____
_____.

C. Imagine that different friends and family members all want you to do something for them today. Using one of the words in the box, write a sentence about why it would be good to be philosophical in this situation.

philosophical philosophy

_____
_____
_____

Critical Vocabulary

trappings	upbringing	depriving	dismantled
waning	liberation	caste	oppression

A. Write the word from the box for each definition.

1. the rearing and training received during childhood _____

2. a social class that is hereditary _____

3. took apart, disassembled _____

4. the process of setting free _____

5. decreasing in size, number, or strength _____

B. Complete each sentence with the correct word from the box.

1. Gandhi's mother taught him to lead a simple life and warned him about the _____ of materialism.

2. Laws were passed in South Africa _____ people of their civil rights.

3. The _____ system in India ranked people by their social class.

4. The British felt their power _____, and arrested Gandhi.

5. Gandhi now stands as a symbol both against the _____ of people and for preaching tolerance, brotherhood, and forgiveness.

C. Choose three words from the box and use each word in a sentence.

1. _____

_____

2. _____

_____

3. _____

_____

Collaborative Discussion Support

As you reread the selection, focus on the answers to these questions.

1. What obstacles did Gandhi overcome in his life?

- _____
- _____
- _____
- _____
- _____
- _____
- _____
- _____

2. Which of these obstacles do you think was the most difficult? Why?

_____

_____

_____

_____

_____

3. What were some of Gandhi's achievements?

- _____
- _____
- _____
- _____
- _____
- _____

4. Which of Gandhi's achievements contributed most to his legacy? What text evidence supports your answer?

_____

_____

_____

_____

_____

Build Vocabulary

Compound Words

upper-class	countryside	play-acting	nationwide
homemade	overthrow	humankind	

A. Choose a word from the box to answer each question.

1. Which word means "theatrical or insincere behavior"? _____

2. Which word means "a rural area"? _____

3. Which word means "to remove someone or something by force"? _____

4. Which word means "the human race"? _____

5. Which word means "including all parts of a nation or country"? _____

B. Complete each sentence with a word from the box.

1. Adele loved the _____ sweater especially because her grandmother knit it.

2. The city conducted a _____ search for a new police chief.

3. Many _____ people simply don't understand what it is like to be poor.

4. Tired of _____, Alan decided to tell the truth about the missing computer.

5. In the summer, Marisa leaves the city and stays at her house in the _____.

C. Choose three words from the box. Use each word in a sentence.

1. _____

_____

_____

2. _____

_____

_____

3. _____

_____

_____

Speak Out! Support

Focus on the answers to these questions as you prepare for your discussion.

What are the advantages and disadvantages of Gandhi's nonviolent approach?

Advantages	Text Evidence Support
_____	_____
_____	_____
_____	_____
_____	_____
_____	_____

Disadvantages	Text Evidence Support
_____	_____
_____	_____
_____	_____
_____	_____
_____	_____

How did Gandhi's legacy inspire the following people?

Martin Luther King: _____

_____

_____

Nelson Mandela: _____

_____

_____

Aung San Suu Kyi: _____

_____

_____

Visual Clues

| public speaking | prejudice | dedicated | urging | arrested |

A. Choose the best answer from the box to complete each sentence.

1. Hector has _____ himself to helping the homeless in the city.

2. At her best friend's _____, Kim decided to volunteer at the soup kitchen.

3. The young woman was _____ shortly after she robbed the convenience store.

4. Many people have a fear of _____.

B. Write the word from the box that most closely fits each of the following descriptions of an illustration.

1. Gandhi is speaking in front of a crowd of people, his left hand raised in the air perhaps to emphasize a point. He is saying, "Down with Britain." _____

2. Gandhi is speaking in front of a judge, looking very frightened. The words he speaks show that he is struggling to speak clearly. _____

3. Gandhi is standing between two soldiers, waiting for the judge to give him his sentence.

   _____

4. In the train, Gandhi is sitting up front. In the back an angry man is complaining about Gandhi being on the train. _____

C. Choose three words from the box. Use each word in a sentence that is not about Gandhi.

1. _____

   _____

2. _____

   _____

3. _____

   _____

Prepositional Phrases

A. Decide if the prepositional phrase in each prompt is acting as an adverb of place, an adverb of time, an adverb of manner, or an adverb of cause. Circle the correct answer.

1. Jameel always dresses formally because his father insists that it's necessary.

   a. place   **b.** time   **c.** manner   **d.** cause

2. Nicky laughs like a hyena.

   a. place   **b.** time   **c.** manner   **d.** cause

3. The gate will open at midnight.

   a. place   **b.** time   **c.** manner   **d.** cause

4. I found Megan beside the lake.

   a. place   **b.** time   **c.** manner   **d.** cause

B. Fill in the blank with a <u>preposition</u> that fits.

1. My father's voice echoed _____ the hall.

2. Boris leaned _____ the rail.

3. Dr. Isaacson teaches poetry _____ his love of language.

4. This machine is powered _____ sunlight.

5. Kim felt sick _____ lunch.

C. Choose one topic and write at least four sentences about it. The paragraph must include at least three prepositional phrases used as adverbs. Possible topics:

details on a meeting	ways different people talk	reasons to be kind to other people

1. _____

   _____

2. _____

   _____

3. _____

   _____

4. _____

   _____

Writing Activity: Search Terms

Read the Performance Task on Student Book page 213 to complete this page.

Part A: Choose Search Terms

List possible search terms that you could use to find the information about Gandhi's achievements while he lived in South Africa.

- _____
- _____
- _____
- _____
- _____
- _____
- _____
- _____

Part B: Review the Search Results

1. One at a time, type your sets of search terms into a search engine. Which of the results will you select? Why?

   _____
   _____
   _____
   _____

2. What are three ways you can check to see if information from a website is trustworthy?

   _____
   _____
   _____
   _____

   Write any other notes about how you will decide on search terms, review search results, and decide what information you will choose.

   _____
   _____
   _____
   _____

The Prefixes *dis*– and *re*–

| discrimination | disobedience | dismantle | return | remember | reflected | response |

A. Choose a word from the box to answer each question.

1. Which word means "an oral or written reply to a question"? _____

2. Which word means "to destroy something in an orderly way"? _____

3. Which word means "to cause something or a thought to come back into your mind"?

   _____

4. Which word means "the practice of treating a person or a group of people differently than

   other people"? _____

5. Which word means "to come or go to a place again"? _____

B. Complete each sentence with a word from the box.

1. Civil _____ is a way of protesting unfair laws.

2. As Amanda _____ on her own behavior, she decided that she would stop

   making fun of other people.

3. Luisa planned to _____ to her hometown during the summer.

4. Marco's _____ to the question was too long and hard to follow.

5. Marisa tried very hard to _____ where she left her keys but had no idea where

   she put them.

C. Choose five words from the box. Use each word in a sentence.

1. _____

   _____

2. _____

   _____

3. _____

   _____

4. _____

   _____

5. _____

   _____

Choose a Topic for a Research Report

After researching the topic of landmark Supreme Court decisions on the Internet, choose three or four decisions that you would like to know more about. List the decisions and the sources for your information (the complete URL).

_____

_____

_____

_____

_____

_____

Narrow your search for information about each of the decisions you have listed. What did you find interesting about each topic?

Decision 1 _____

What I found interesting was _____

_____

Decision 2 _____

What I found interesting was _____

_____

Decision 3 _____

What I found interesting was _____

_____

Decision 4 _____

What I found interesting was _____

_____

Which decision will you choose to write about? Why?

_____

_____

_____

_____

_____

_____

Academic Vocabulary

Make an Outline

After you gather your sources, take notes, and check your facts, use the outline below to plan your research report.

Main Idea

Write the main idea for your research report.

_____

_____

_____

Supporting Details

What details will you use to support your main idea?

A. Supporting detail: _____

_____

B. Supporting detail: _____

_____

C. Supporting detail: _____

_____

What text evidence from the sources can you use?

_____

_____

_____

What primary and secondary sources will you use?

_____

_____

_____

What are some ideas for the title of your research report?

_____

_____

_____

Academic Vocabulary

A. Complete each sentence with the correct word from the box.

published	publisher

1. Sonia Sotomayor has _____ a book about her life before she became a judge.

public	publication

2. After the _____ of the book, Judge Sotomayor appeared on television shows to talk about it.

publisher	publish

3. A _____ printed and distributed the book.

public	publishing

4. In the book, she tells the _____ about what her life was like growing up in New York.

B. Read the passage and answer the questions.

> In the past, authors mailed copies of their typed stories to publishers. Then they sat at home waiting to get a letter telling them if the publisher would accept the story or not. Now, there are more different kinds of publications—ebooks and webzines. Authors can easily publish their own stories for sale on the Internet.

1. In the past, where did authors mail their typed stories?

In they past, authors mailed _____.

2. What kinds of new publications are there now?

Now, there are _____.

3. How can authors publish and sell their own stories?

Authors can easily _____.

C. Using a word from the box, write a sentence telling about how or where you would publish a text you have written.

publish	publisher	publication

_____

Finalize Your Plan

WRITING TOOLBOX

Elements of a Research Essay

Introduction	In the introduction, present your main idea. Include an interesting fact, question, or quotation.
Main Idea and Details	You can have one paragraph or more than one. If you have more than one, each paragraph should include a main idea and supporting details.
Conclusion	The conclusion should follow and sum up how the details support your main idea.
Bibliography	A bibliography is a list of sources that you have consulted or cited in your report.

A. Review the elements of a research essay above. Describe the elements that you will use in your report.

Introduction _____

_____

Main Idea and Details _____

_____

Conclusion _____

_____

Bibliography _____

_____

_____

B. Write a brief summary of your essay.

_____

_____

_____

_____

Build Vocabulary

Vocabulary Review

Here are some of the words you learned in this unit. Choose words from this list and sort them into the categories below. There are many possible correct answers! Also, many of the words fit into more than one category.

achievements	communication	homemade	overthrow	solo
autobiography	complacent	humankind	philosophy	strike
beaming	countryside	inheritance	precedent	testimony
bequest	dedicated	liberation	prodigy	transcended
birthright	discrimination	memoir	protest	tolerance
cases	dismantle	nationwide	reflected	uncomfortable
caste	dissents	opinions	return	uniform
communicable	heritage	oppressive	segregation	upper-class

Nouns
1. _____
2. _____
3. _____
4. _____

Compound Words
1. _____
2. _____
3. _____
4. _____

Words with Prefixes
1. _____
2. _____
3. _____
4. _____

Synonyms of "Legacy"
1. _____
2. _____
3. _____

Easily Confused Words

A. Decide which word best completes each sentence. Circle the correct answer.

1. Make sure to _____ your sources when you write a research paper.

   a. sight   **b.** site   **c.** cite   **d.** patience

2. It takes a lot of _____ to get good at fishing.

   a. sight   **b.** site   **c.** patience   **d.** patients

3. The detective reached the _____ where the accident happened.

   a. cite   **b.** site   **c.** patience   **d.** patients

4. The skilled nurse could take care of a dozen _____ all by herself.

   a. sight   **b.** site   **c.** patience   **d.** patients

B. Fill in the blank with a word that fits.

1. Luna laughed at the _____ of her little brother with a bucket stuck on his head.

2. The researcher got in trouble because he didn't _____ an important fact.

3. They're going to build a hotel at this _____ .

4. Try to have the _____ to finish the job.

5. The hospital was full of _____ on Friday night.

C. Choose one topic and write four sentences about it. Use at least three of the following words: *site, sight, cite, patients, patience*. Possible topics:

doing research on where to build a hospital	doing research in the place where a famous historical event happened	something beautiful that you have to wait a lot to see, like a sunset

1. _____

   _____

2. _____

   _____

3. _____

   _____

4. _____

   _____

The Value of Work

"... gardens are not made by singing 'Oh, how beautiful!' and sitting in the shade."

— Rudyard Kipling, author

What comes to your mind when you think of the value of work? You can draw or make written notes.

What are some kinds of work?

_____

_____

If you enjoy doing a job, is it still work? Why or why not?

_____

_____

Is a volunteer job still work? Why or why not?

_____

_____

Write your own definition of *work*. You will review it at the end of this unit.

_____

_____

Other notes about the value of work:

_____

_____

_____

_____

Academic Vocabulary

As you work through Unit 6, look and listen for these words. Practice using them when you talk in class and in your writing. Write about your experiences using these words in the last column of the chart.

Word	Definition	Related Forms	My Experiences
commentary	explanation or interpretation—in the form of comments	comment, commentator	
minors	people who have not yet reached legal adulthood	minor, minority	
occupation	a job or profession	occupy, occupational	
option	a choice	optional, opt	
style	• a way of doing something • a certain design or form • fashion sense	stylistic, stylistically, stylish	

Idioms

Write a sentence using each idiom below. Make sure a reader can understand the meaning of that idiom from your sentence.

1. To work like a dog

_____

_____

_____

2. To hit the books

_____

_____

_____

3. To roll up one's sleeves

_____

_____

_____

4. To call it a day

_____

_____

_____

5. To burn the midnight oil

_____

_____

_____

6. To knuckle down

_____

_____

_____

7. To talk shop

_____

_____

_____

The Meaning of Work

Use the Performance Task instructions on page 221 of the Student Book to complete this page.

A. Think about what the word *work* means to you. Then brainstorm examples of work in two categories:

1. What kinds of work seem like chores?

   _____

2. What kinds of work seem absorbing and rewarding?

   _____

B. Use your examples to write your paragraph. You will explain why your definition of *work* makes the most sense.

1. Start with a topic sentence that explains your opinion about the word *work*.

   _____

   _____

   _____

2. Offer two or more examples to support your opinion.

   _____

   _____

   _____

3. Explain why another definition of *work* just doesn't make sense.

   _____

   _____

   _____

4. End the paragraph by repeating your main point—your opinion about work.

   _____

   _____

   _____

5. Be sure to revise your paragraph, as needed, and check your spelling and grammar.

   _____

   _____

   _____

Collaborative Discussion Support

Complete these charts while reviewing "The Network Kid" on Student Book pages 222–223.

Why did The Network Kid publish this blog?	Cite text evidence.	What do you know about this from your own experiences?
_____ _____ _____	_____ _____ _____	_____ _____ _____
_____ _____ _____	_____ _____ _____	_____ _____ _____
_____ _____ _____	_____ _____ _____	_____ _____ _____

Why would The Network Kid maintain this blog?	Cite text evidence, if possible.	What do you know about this from your own experiences?
_____ _____ _____	_____ _____ _____	_____ _____ _____
_____ _____ _____	_____ _____ _____	_____ _____ _____

What kinds of jobs could eighth graders do? Put a star beside the ones that you would enjoy.
_____ _____

Use with the Collaborative Discussion on **Student Book** page 224.

Critical Vocabulary

A. Read the sentences below. Circle the definition of each underlined word. Remember that you can look up any unfamiliar words in the dictionary.

1. Most job applications require a <u>resume</u>. A *resume* is _____.

   a. a job posting.   **b.** a list of experience.   **c.** a personal website.

2. I am <u>employed</u> full time. *Employed* means _____.

   a. hired and working.   **b.** without a regular job.   **c.** not working.

3. I want to work and live an <u>independent</u> lifestyle. *Independent* means _____.

   a. rich.   **b.** not depending on anyone else.   **c.** carefree.

4. We <u>brainstormed</u> different plans regarding how to start a successful job search. *Brainstormed* means _____.

   a. thought of ideas.   **b.** wrote down.   **c.** picked and chose.

B. Choose a word from the box to complete each sentence.

resume	reference	independent	participated	brainstormed	employed

1. I listed all my recent experience on my _____.

2. I asked my boss if I could use her as a _____ when I apply for jobs.

3. Having a job makes you feel _____.

4. I _____ in a job fair last year.

5. We _____ some ideas on what jobs to look for.

C. Choose three words from the box in Part B. Use each word in a sentence.

1. _____

   _____

2. _____

   _____

3. _____

   _____

Write a Resume

Read the Write On! prompt on page 224 of the Student Book before working on this page.

1. List your responsibilities and any past job experience. Start with your most recent one.

Job/responsibility _____ dates _____ to _____

What you did _____

_____

_____

Job/responsibility _____ dates _____ to _____

What you did _____

_____

_____

Job/responsibility _____ dates _____ to _____

What you did _____

_____

_____

Job/responsibility _____ dates _____ to _____

What you did _____

_____

_____

2. List your skills, such as being well-organized, careful with details, and able to solve problems. Describe some examples of times where you needed these skills.

_____

_____

3. Describe your education.

Grade in school: _____

Courses taken inside or outside school that helped prepare you for a job: _____

_____

_____

4. List your interests and hobbies that apply to getting a job.

_____

_____

_____

Sharing Blogs

To evaluate your blog, use the Blog Rubric available from your online Student Resources or from your teacher. This page will help you prepare to respond to other blogs and to encourage other bloggers to respond to yours.

1. **Respond to other bloggers.**

   List at least three blogs you already know that you will respond to. Be sure to mention your own blog, so these bloggers can respond to you.

   a. _____

   _____

   b. _____

   _____

   c. _____

   _____

2. **Find new blogs.**

   List at least three new blogs that interest you and you will respond to. You might make one of them a community online blog.

   a. _____

   _____

   b. _____

   _____

   c. _____

   _____

3. **Invite your readers to respond to you and to suggest future topics.**

   What kinds of questions can you include in your blog that will encourage others to respond? How can you encourage others to suggest future topics?

   a. _____

   _____

   b. _____

   _____

   c. _____

   _____

   d. _____

   _____

Multiple-Meaning Words

A. Choose the response that correctly defines the underlined word. Circle the correct answer.

1. Hector was thrilled to have landed a job in a local grocery <u>store</u>.

    a. a place where things are sold   **b.** put something that is not being used in a certain place

2. It was a beautiful day, so we decided to go to the <u>park</u>.

    a. leave a truck or car in a particular place

    b. a piece of land where people can exercise or relax

3. My father leaves for <u>work</u> at 5:00 a.m.

    a. do something for which you will be paid   **b.** the place where you go to do your job

4. I'm applying for a job. Would you mind writing a <u>reference</u> for me?

    a. mention someone in a speech or writing

    b. a statement attesting to someone's skills and/or character

B. Define each underlined word.

1. We will <u>park</u> the car about a mile away from the stadium.

_____

2. Scientist are investigating how the brain <u>stores</u> memories.

_____

3. The <u>school</u> of fish swam straight past us.

_____

4. Amanda gave an incorrect <u>reference</u> in her term paper.

_____

C. Choose three words from the box. Use each word in two sentences that show different meanings of the word.

work	reference	school	store	park

1. _____

_____

2. _____

_____

3. _____

_____

Clauses

A. Multiple Choice. Decide if the dependent clause in the sentence functions as an adjective or an adverb. Circle the correct answer.

1. My dad, whose father was from Nigeria, grew up in the United States.

   a. whose father was from Nigera, adverb clause

   b. whose father was from Nigeria, adjective clause

2. Ilyas speaks to his mother in Arabic at home.

   a. Ilyas speaks to his mother, adjective clause

   b. This sentence has no dependent clause.

3. The long article that I read yesterday was more interesting than I expected.

   a. that I read yesterday, adverb clause

   b. that I read yesterday, adjective clause

4. The speaker presented his story where everybody could hear her.

   a. where everybody could hear her, adverb clause

   b. where everybody could hear her, adjective clause

B. Fill in the blank with a clause that fits.

1. The woman _____ dog shows loves her job.

2. The argument _____ surprised me.

3. A dog _____ can be a great friend

4. Sam can work _____ .

5. The baseball players practiced _____ .

C. Write four sentences about a topic. Two must include adjective clauses, and two must include adverb clauses. Possible topics are listed below, or you may use your own.

waiting for something	completing homework	identifying someone

1. _____

2. _____

3. _____

4. _____

Information

Answer the questions about *Summer Jobs*.

1. What are Rashida and Jerome doing in this video?

_____

_____

2. Where did Rashida work for her summer job?

_____

_____

3. What were some of her tasks?

_____

_____

4. How did her summer job influence what she wants to do in the future?

_____

_____

5. Where did Jerome work for his summer job?

_____

_____

6. Why did he like it especially this year?

_____

_____

Compare and Contrast

Think about the video you have just seen. Compare and contrast it with "The Network Kid."

1. What common topic do the video and the blog share?

_____

_____

2. What's the main difference between the video and the blog?

_____

_____

3. What kind of summer job would interest you? Explain.

_____

_____

Critical Vocabulary

A. Circle four words in the Word Bank that you want to know more about.

Word Bank

supplement	sufficient	diminished	rewarding	maintain	commentary	serenity
botany	challenging	differentiate	unique	genus	transforming	

B. Watch the video *Summer Jobs* again and listen for the words. Complete the activity.

1. Word: _____

What I think it means: _____

What it means: _____

2. Word: _____

What I think it means: _____

What it means: _____

3. Word: _____

What I think it means: _____

What it means: _____

4. Word: _____

What I think it means: _____

What it means: _____

C. Choose three words that you wrote in Part B. Write a sentence using each word.

1. _____

_____

_____

2. _____

_____

_____

3. _____

_____

_____

Academic Vocabulary

A. Complete each sentence with the correct word from the box.

1. Dr. Martin is a sports _____ who appears frequently on television.

comment	commentator

2. The official refused to _____ on the reporter's question.

commentary	comment

3. There has been a lot of _____ about the new education law.

commentator	commentary

4. June's positive _____ about Nick's article made his day.

comments	commentator

B. Read the passage and answer the questions.

> George and Lizette are going to a meeting to discuss some new school rules. The school will consider the group's comments before the rules become final. The principal will give her commentary first so that everyone understands why they want to make the new rules. Afterward, other people can comment on what she said.

1. What will the school consider before the rules become final?

The school will consider _____.

2. What will the principal do first?

The principal _____.

3. What can other people do after the principal speaks?

Afterwards, other people _____.

C. If a reporter asked you for a comment on the last book you read, what would you say? Give your answer in a complete sentence using a word from the box.

comment	commentary

Name of the book: _____

_____

Critical Vocabulary

A. Read these sentences from "Interview with Babe Secoli." Circle the definition of each underlined word. Remember that you can look up any unfamiliar words in the dictionary.

1. I can't be bothered with their little <u>trifles</u> because I have another customer who needs help. *Trifles* are

   a. important issues.　　**b.** trivial problems.　　**c.** difficult situations.

2. Right now I'm ready for <u>retirement</u> as far as the union goes. *Retirement* is

   a. not working.　　**b.** getting a raise.　　**c.** getting a promotion.

3. What <u>irritates</u> me is when customers get very cocky with me. *Irritates* means

   a. pleases.　　**b.** annoys.　　**c.** saddens.

4. I'm not <u>ashamed</u> that I wear a uniform and nursing shoes and that I have varicose veins. *Ashamed* means

   a. happy.　　**b.** angry.　　**c.** embarrassed.

B. Choose a word from the box to complete each sentence.

discount	automatically	retirement	ashamed
irritates	infallible	extent	trifles

1. If you're lucky at the store, you might find items on _____.

2. Everybody makes mistakes because no one is _____.

3. That brief conversation was the _____ of our interaction.

4. I am saving money for _____.

5. I _____ know the cost of all the items in the store at first sight.

C. Choose three words from the box in Part B. Use each word in a sentence.

1. _____

_____

2. _____

_____

3. _____

_____

Collaborative Discussion Support

Review "Interview with Babe Secoli" on Student Book pp. 227–230 to complete the charts below.

Is Babe's language in this excerpt formal or informal? How do you know?	Cite text evidence or clues.
_____	_____
_____	_____
_____	_____
_____	_____
_____	_____
_____	_____

How does the author's choice to use Babe's voice authentically affect the quality of the story?
_____
_____
_____

What evidence in the text gives you a sense of Babe's character and values?	Cite text evidence or clues.
_____	_____
_____	_____
_____	_____
_____	_____
_____	_____
_____	_____

Use with the Collaborative Discussion on **Student Book** page 231.

Multiple-Meaning Words

A. Use context clues to choose the best answer. Circle the answer.

1. If I don't <u>find</u> my glasses I will be seriously in trouble. In this sentence, *find* means

   a. treasure.   **b.** locate.

2. My watch won't <u>run</u> unless you wind it. A synonym for *run* is

   a. work.   **b.** race.

3. She needed to <u>break</u> a ten-dollar bill. In this sentence *break* means

   a. to crush.   **b.** to exchange.

4. They're planning to <u>shoot</u> a commercial on my block. In this sentence *shoot* has to do with

   a. photography.   **b.** weaponry.

5. My dog will eat vegetables if they're <u>ground</u>. In this sentence *ground* means

   a. crushed.   **b.** dry land.

B. Write new sentences for the words below. Get the meanings from your answers in Part A.

1. find _____

2. run _____

3. break _____

4. shoot _____

5. ground _____

C. Write sentences for three of the underlined words from Part A using the meanings you *didn't* choose in Part B. Use a dictionary or thesaurus if needed.

1. _____

   _____

   _____

2. _____

   _____

   _____

3. _____

   _____

   _____

Performance Task

Conduct an Interview

Follow the steps below to conduct an interview that will become part of a narrative.

Step 1: Choose an interviewee.

You might ask to interview a family member, neighbor, or adult friend.

The people I will ask are: _____.

This person agreed to be interviewed: _____

Our interview is set for this day: _____ at this time: _____.

Step 2: Make a list of questions to ask this person.

You will probably think of more questions during the interview. Remember that an interview is a conversation, so you have to adapt and introduce more questions as you learn more information.

_____

_____

_____

_____

_____

_____

Step 3: Carry out your interview.

Step 4: Send your interviewee a written thank-you note.

Write Your Narrative

Step 1: Organize your notes under headings. You might decide not to include the headings in your narrative, but they will help you get organized.

I will use these headings: _____

Step 2: Write a draft of your narrative on another sheet of paper.

Step 3: Edit and revise your narrative.

If possible, have a partner read your edited version and suggest any needed changes.
Then write your final draft.

Step 4: Share your narrative with a partner, a small group, or the class.

Compound Words

high school	everything	typewriter	second wind	shoplifter	somewhere

A. Choose a word from the box to answer each question.

1. What word means "someone who steals from a store while pretending to be a customer"?

   _____

2. What word means "all that exists"? _____

3. What word means "a school that includes grades 9–12 or 10–12"? _____

4. What word means "a machine that prints letters or figures on a sheet of paper when a person pushes on its keys"? _____

5. What means "in, at, or to a place that is not known or specified"? _____

B. Complete each sentence with a word from the box at the top of the page.

1. The computer has pretty much replaced the _____ for writing letters and documents.

2. After swimming seven laps in the pool and getting tired, Alva finally got her _____ and kept going.

3. The _____ was caught stealing and was asked to return the objects.

4. Ramon ate _____ that was on his plate because he was so hungry after playing basketball all afternoon.

5. My missing book has got to be _____ in the house; I know I didn't lose it.

C. Choose three words from the box at the top of the page. Use each word in a sentence.

1. _____

   _____

   _____

2. _____

   _____

   _____

3. _____

   _____

   _____

Compound Sentences

A. Decide what the underlined <u>coordinating conjunction</u> does in the sentence. Circle the correct answer.

1. The meeting starts very soon, <u>and</u> I'm running late.

    a. joins two similar ideas   **b.** shows contrast, opposition, or difference

2. Naomi figured out how to fix the boat, <u>so</u> we'll go out on the lake soon.

    a. joins two similar ideas   **b.** tells why something is or what resulted from something

3. The engine is making a weird noise, <u>but</u> Ed says it's safe.

    a. joins two similar ideas   **b.** shows contrast, opposition, or difference

4. Joe can either grill burgers <u>or</u> roast vegetables.

    a. joins two similar ideas   **b.** shows a choice or an alternative

B. Complete each sentence with a coordinating conjunction.

    1. The game is nearly over, _____ Marcel wants to stop watching.

    2. Isaiah is the strongest guy I know, _____ even he can't lift that box.

    3. Clara kicked the door open, _____ the sound made everyone in the room jump.

    4. Jane hates to pace herself—she either runs as fast as she can _____ doesn't run at all.

    5. Mr. Munoz has better eyesight than me, _____ I asked him to watch the road for me.

C. Choose one topic and write four sentences about it. Use at least three of the following coordinating conjunctions: *and, or, so, but*. Possible topics:

deciding which way to go while lost in a cave	traveling to a distant relative's house	deciding what to cook for a dinner with friends

1. _____

_____

2. _____

_____

3. _____

_____

4. _____

_____

Collaborative Discussion Support

Complete these charts to prepare to discuss "The Village Blacksmith" on Student Book pages 232–234.

Discussing the Purpose

What words and phrases does the poet use to help you imagine scenes from the poem?

Words or phrases	Line in poem	Image in my mind

Comparing Texts

Think about how Terkel and Longfellow wrote about work.

How did Terkel address the concept of work?

_____

_____

What style did Terkel use in the excerpt you read?

_____

_____

What clues in the poem indicate how Longfellow felt about work?

_____

_____

What style did Longfellow use in this poem?

_____

_____

Use with the Collaborative Discussion on **Student Book** page 235.

Academic Vocabulary

A. Complete each sentence with the correct word from the box.

1. The errors in this document are only _____.

minor	minority

2. It's sometimes hard to get a group of people to do what you want when you are in the

_____.

minor	minority

3. When _____ travel by airplane, the airline often provides special care for them.

minors	minorities

B. Read the passage and answer the questions.

> All of the political parties in the United States are trying to attract minority voters. The Hispanic population is large, but many of them are minors. When they get old enough to vote, they may be the ones to decide which party is in the majority, and that is not a minor detail.

1. Who are the political parties trying to attract?

They are trying _____.

2. What are many Hispanics now?

Many Hispanics _____.

3. What is not a minor detail?

It is not a minor detail that when Hispanics get old enough, they may

_____.

C. Using the word *minor*, write a sentence about the benefits of being a minor.

_____

_____

_____

_____

Analyzing the Text

Complete this chart to analyze "The Village Blacksmith," Student Book pages 232–234. Read Student Book page 235 for guidance on making inferences. Include explicit text citations to support your answers.

Make Inferences	Cite text evidence
What does Longfellow explicitly say about blacksmiths in the first two stanzas of the poem?	
What does Longfellow imply about blacksmiths in these two stanzas?	
In the last stanza, Longfellow thanks blacksmiths for the lesson they teach us. What lesson does he have in mind? Make an inference and support it with text evidence.	

Use the information for Analyzing the Text on **Student Book** page 235.

Context Clues

A. Answer each question about the underlined word. Circle the correct answer.

1. If a young man has <u>brawny</u> arms, what do his arms look like?

    a. They are muscular.   **b.** They are covered with tattoos.

2. If an event makes you <u>rejoice</u>, how does the event make you feel?

    a. happy   **b.** worried

3. What would a blacksmith use a <u>sledge</u> for?

    a. to take the metal in and out of the forge   **b.** to pound metal into a certain shape

4. If you are in a state of <u>repose</u>, what are you doing?

    a. trying to solve a problem   **b.** resting or sleeping

B. Complete each sentence with the correct word from the box.

brawny	sledge	forge	rejoice	repose

1. If you hit a glass bowl with a _____, it will shatter.

2. All we could do was _____ when our team won the Super Bowl.

3. The _____ emitted an intense heat.

4. With his _____ physique, Carlos easily lifted the massive rock and brought it to the side of the road.

C. Choose three words from the box. Use each word in a sentence.

1. _____

_____

_____

2. _____

_____

_____

3. _____

_____

_____

Summarize the Podcast

As you listen to the podcast, pay attention to the main points and write them in this chart. Later, you might narrow the main points you listed to three or four important ones.

Use with the discussion of a summary on **Student Book** page 237.

Discuss these questions with your group and then write your answers to prepare for the class discussion on Student Book page 237.

1. How does Chris Hadfield think you should set goals?

_____

_____

_____

_____

2. How does this apply to people your age?

_____

_____

_____

_____

3. What if you learn that your "dream job" isn't exactly what you expected, that you've been having a "distortion of reality"? Then what should you do?

_____

_____

_____

_____

4. How can you be "victorious on a daily basis"?

_____

_____

_____

_____

5. Why is it important to have small victories?

_____

_____

_____

_____

Reference Aids: Dictionaries

A. Answer the questions about the dictionary entry below.

> orbit (ôr'bĭt) n.
>
> 1. the path that a planet or other object takes as it circles another
>
> **orbital adj.**
>
> From Latin *orbita*—path

1. What part of speech is "orbit"? _____

2. What related word does the entry show? _____

3. How many syllables does "orbit" have? _____

4. What is the origin of the word *orbit*? _____

B. The words in the box are from the podcast "Chris Hadfield on the Future of Manned Space Exploration." Choose two words that you would like to know more about. Look them up in a dictionary. Provide information about each entry.

orbit	erosion	degraded	distortion	fanciful	qualifications

1. Word: _____

   Part of Speech: _____

   Definition: _____

   _____

2. Word: _____

   Part of Speech: _____

   Definition: _____

   _____

C. Use each word you looked up in Part B in a sentence. Underline the words you looked up.

1. _____

   _____

2. _____

   _____

Compound-Complex Sentences

A. Identify the subordinate conjunction and the coordinating conjunction in the sentence. Circle the correct answer.

1. As the day got hotter, we got tired, so we rested in the shade.

   a. As and we   **b.** As and so   **c.** we and so   **d.** we and in

2. Marlene made a campfire while her friends explored and was cooking fish by the time they got back.

   a. while and and   **b.** while and by   **c.** and and by   **d.** by and back

3. Dan can fix the computer whenever you bring it to him, so there's no need to hurry.

   a. can and whenever   **b.** whenever and to   **c.** whenever and so   **d.** so and no

4. The scientist can take the readings when the sun goes down, or she can wait until dawn.

   a. can and when   **b.** can and down   **c.** when and or   **d.** when and dawn

B. Fill in the blank with a word that fits.

1. The bell will be ringing _____ someone shuts it off, so it's best to ignore it.

2. The relay race is about to start, while the marathon is already going on, _____ I can't decide which to watch.

3. The game won't start _____ we've picked teams, but that won't take very long.

4. My coach is patient, _____ she looks so disappointed when I'm late, and I really don't want to disappoint her.

5. The pipe is leaking badly, _____ it's above ground level, so we do need a plumber.

C. Choose one topic and write four sentences about it. At least two of the sentences must be <u>compound complex</u> sentences—that is, sentences that use both a subordinate conjunction and a coordinating conjunction. Possible topics:

a problem the protagonist in a story faces	making a difficult choice	deciding how best to help a friend with a problem they have

1. _____

2. _____

3. _____

4. _____

Critical Vocabulary

A. Read the sentences below. Circle the definition of each underlined word. Remember that you can look up any unfamiliar words in the dictionary.

1. Work has a specific meaning and can actually be <u>calculated</u>. *Calculated* means

   a. assessed mathematically.   **b.** estimated.   **c.** hypothesized.

2. In physics, a force <u>applied</u> to an object does work while it changes how an object moves. *Applied* means

   a. detracted from.   **b.** put to use.   **c.** in addition to.

3. Physicists consider the amount of work done to be the product of an object's <u>displacement</u> and the amount of force applied. *Displacement* means

   a. the distance an object is moved.   **b.** out of place.   **c.** put into place.

4. If you haven't made any <u>progress</u> you haven't done any work. *Progress* means

   a. movement backward.   **b.** movement forward.   **c.** static movement.

B. Choose a word from the box to complete each sentence.

task	displacement	applied	measured	calculated	progress

1. The work you put into a _____ has a measurable outcome.

2. I _____ the outcome of my work by looking at what I had accomplished.

3. Physicists study the _____ of objects.

4. In physics, everything is _____ and precise.

5. I _____ force to the ball in order to measure how far it can be pushed.

C. Choose three words from the box in Part B. Use each word in a sentence.

1. _____
   _____

2. _____
   _____

3. _____
   _____

Write an Argument

Read the Performance Task section on page 241 of the Student Book before answering the questions below.

1. Decide where you stand on this question. What is your claim? Must work include measurable progress? Or is effort enough to qualify as work?

   My opinion is that

   _____

   _____

   _____

   _____

   _____

2. Now list the reasons and evidence for your opinion. Be sure to include examples that will convince readers that you are right.

   _____

   _____

   _____

   _____

   _____

   List any counterclaims and explain why they are wrong.

   _____

   _____

   _____

   _____

   _____

3. End with your conclusion. Restate your claim or opinion and summarize the key facts supporting it.

   _____

   _____

   _____

   _____

   _____

Academic Vocabulary

A. Complete each sentence with the correct word from the box.

occupy	occupation	occupational

1. Craig is thinking about going into an _____ in the health care field.

2. During school vacations, it's not hard to find something to _____ your time.

3. _____ therapists help people recover from injuries so that they can do the activities they need for their jobs and daily life.

4. Wei's dream _____ is to become a video game designer.

B. Complete each sentence.

1. After school I will occupy myself by _____.

2. I think that _____ would be a nice occupation because

   _____

   _____

   _____.

C. Using a word from the box, write a sentence about how you will prepare for your future occupation.

_____

_____

_____

_____

_____

_____

_____

_____

_____

_____

_____

_____

_____

Critical Vocabulary

A. Read the sentences below. Circle the definition of each underlined word. Remember that you can look up any unfamiliar words in the dictionary.

1. Choose a stance before you write your argument. A *stance* is

    a. a topic.   **b.** a writing style.   **c.** a point of view.

2. While listening to an argument, see if you can identify the speaker's position on the issue. An *argument* is

    a. a persuasive set of reasons.   **b.** an expository essay.   **c.** the written word.

3. An author's claim should be easy to identify. A *claim* is

    a. a conclusion.   **b.** a kind of paragraph.   **c.** an assertion.

4. Consider the evidence shown in the essay. *Evidence* is

    a. reasons supporting the truth of something.

    b. little known information.

    c. formal language.

5. Listen with an open but sensible mind. *Sensible* means

    a. easily persuaded.   **b.** grounded.   **c.** sensitive.

B. Choose a word from the box to complete each sentence.

evidence	sensible	challenge	argument	stance	claim

1. The work you put into a _____ has a measurable outcome.

2. I _____ the outcome of my work by looking at what I had accomplished.

3. Physicists study the _____ of objects.

4. In physics, everything is _____ and precise.

5. I _____ force to the ball in order to measure how far it can be pushed.

C. Choose three words from the box in Part B. Use each word in a sentence.

1. _____

2. _____

3. _____

Critical Vocabulary

A. Circle the definition of each underlined word. Remember that you can look up any unfamiliar words in the dictionary.

1. Mother Jones supported <u>textile</u> workers. *Textile* is

   a. a type of tile.   **b.** a type of fabric.   **c.** a type of textbook.

2. Jones planned to ask the president to pass a federal law prohibiting the <u>exploitation</u> of child laborers. *Exploitation* means

   a. benefiting from the mistreatment of others.   **b.** revealing injustices.   **c.** striking.

3. Mother Jones fought for higher <u>wages</u>. *Wages* are

   a. benefits.   **b.** payment.   **c.** safety standards.

4. Child <u>labor</u> is unfair and dangerous. *Labor* means

   a. work.   **b.** play.   **c.** education.

B. Choose a word from the box to complete each sentence.

textile	coverage	labor	publicity
exploitation	wages	enforce	instrumental

1. Mother Jones thought holding protests and strikes would be good _____ for the cause.

2. There was little press _____ of the strike.

3. It is important to _____ laws protecting children.

4. The Children's Crusade was an _____ social justice movement.

5. Activists continue to fight against the _____ of children.

C. Choose three words from the box in Part B. Use each word in a sentence.

1. _____

   _____

2. _____

   _____

3. _____

   _____

Etymology

tragedy	factory	publicity	symbolic	prohibiting	labor

A. Choose the correct answer from the words in the box.

1. Which word is formed from a Latin word that means "doer" or "maker"? _____

2. Which word is formed from a Greek word that means "token" or "sign"? _____

3. Which word comes from a Latin word that means "pertaining to the people"? _____

4. Which word is formed from a Latin word that means "toil" or "exertion"? _____

B. Answer the questions with the correct word.

1. Write a word that belongs to the same word family as *symbolic*. _____

2. Write a word that belongs to the same word family as *labor*. _____

3. Write a word that belongs to the same word family as *publicity*. _____

4. Write a word that belongs to the same word family as *prohibiting*. _____

C. Choose two words from the box and look up their Greek or Latin origins in a dictionary or online. Write down the words you chose and their words of origin on the lines below. Next, find two words that belong to the same word family as the words from the box— write them down next to the words of origin.

babble	biceps	lyric	pathetic

_____

_____

_____

_____

_____

_____

_____

Complex Sentences

A. Decide which subordinate conjunction best completes the sentence. Circle the correct answer.

1. _____ Samir is so good at baseball, he always gets picked first when we're making teams.

   a. While   **b.** Although   **c.** If   **d.** Because

2. Luisa suddenly realized how to solve the problem _____ she was out jogging.

   a. while   **b.** although   **c.** if   **d.** because

3. _____ Carmen's still awake, she must not have finished her paper yet.

   a. While   **b.** Although   **c.** If   **d.** Because

4. We ran out of gas, _____ Wally insisted on driving by a longer route than normal.

   a. while   **b.** although   **c.** if   **d.** because

B. Fill in the blank with a subordinate conjunction that fits.

1. Malcolm couldn't feel his hand _____ he held it in ice water for a minute.

2. Tanya will be under stress _____ she finishes writing her programming project.

3. She's nearly done, _____ there's a bug that keeps reappearing.

4. The sound of buzzing mosquitoes was constant, _____ it was coming from inside my head.

5. Mark will be late, _____ he has to dig his car out of the snow.

C. Choose one topic and write four sentences about it. Use at least three different subordinate conjunctions. Possible topics:

getting good at a new skill	using a computer or other tool that isn't working very well	people at work

1. _____

2. _____

3. _____

4. _____

Collaborative Discussion Support

Complete the following chart. Some boxes have been filled in for you.

Page & ¶s	Problems	Ways Mother Jones Solved Them or Tried to Solve Them
p. 243 ¶ 1	A textile workers' strike in Philadelphia was not getting enough publicity.	She organized a 100-mile march by 100 children who were textile workers.
p. 243 ¶ 2	Mine and factory owners were greedy and unscrupulous.	
p. 244 ¶ 1	Some workers weren't brave enough to stand up for their rights.	
p. 244 ¶ 3		Mother Jones decided to change people's minds about child labor.
p. 244 ¶ 4	Some children had been injured or disabled in factories.	
p. 245 ¶ 1	Most children could not walk the whole distance.	
p. 245 ¶ 1		When the children got to each place, their leaders would arrange food and lodging for them at the last minute.
p. 292 ¶		Jones used the president's refusal to get more sympathy from the public.

Make an Argument

To evaluate your speech, use the Presenting a Speech Rubric available from your online Student Resources or from your teacher.

A. Plan Your Argument

1. Scan "Mother Jones and the Children's Crusade" for "evil" aspects of child labor. List these in your own words: _____

_____

_____

_____

2. Suppose someone argued that families needed their children's wages in order to survive. What would you say to disprove this? _____

_____

_____

_____

3. Suppose someone else said that if children could not work, the crime rate would go up. What would you say to disprove this? _____

_____

_____

_____

4. Instead of working in factories or mines, what could children do with their "spare" time? _____

_____

_____

_____

B. Write Your Argument

Use your notes from Part A to write your argument on another sheet of paper. If you like, you can copy your final draft onto index cards to make your argument easier to present. Remember to use enthusiastic, vivid language and to include the following:

1. **an opening statement** that tells exactly what you are arguing for (such as making it illegal for children under a certain age to work)

2. **reasons** why you support this position and **facts** to support your reasons

3. **a closing statement** that sums up your argument

Build Vocabulary

Academic Vocabulary

A. Complete each sentence with the correct word from the box.

opt	optional

1. Sabrina's mother said, "Go to bed now. Sleep is not _____."

optional	options

2. Erik and Jon were having trouble deciding what to order for lunch. There were so many _____.

option	opt

3. Sometimes we face difficult decisions. Do we _____ for the easy path or the right path?

option	optional

4. When you wake up and see that everything is covered with snow, the only _____ is to start shoveling.

B. Complete each sentence.

1. If I could choose any superpower to have, I would opt to _____

_____.

2. If I am filling out a form and I see (*optional*) under one of the blanks, it means that _____

_____.

C. Using one of the words in the box, write two sentences about your plans for life after you finish school.

opt	option

1. _____

_____

2. _____

_____

Critical Vocabulary

A. Circle the definition of each underlined word. Remember that you can look up any unfamiliar words in the dictionary.

1. I use two different metals for my <u>pendulums</u>—they expand at different rates. *Pendulums* are

   a. swinging weights that regulate a clock.   **b.** clock hands.   **c.** grandfather clocks

2. He was trained as a <u>carpenter</u> and knew how to make material out of wood. A *carpenter* is

   a. an engineer.   **b.** a person who makes wooden objects.

   c. an engineer who works only on ships.

3. Edinburgh and Moscow are two cities on the same <u>latitude</u>. *Latitude* is

   a. the northern-most parts of the world.

   b. imaginary lines running north and south of the equator.   **c.** a certain kind of map.

4. You must look at the lines running up and down to find the <u>longitude</u> points on a map. *Longitude* is

   a. imaginary lines running through the North and South Poles.

   b. a way of measuring very hot or cold temperatures.   **c.** northern state lines.

B. Choose a word from the box to complete each sentence.

carpenter	smallpox	pendulums	foremost
navigation	longitude	latitude	precise

1. Explorers often unknowingly spread _____ to new lands.

2. Mapmakers must know the _____ location of different countries.

3. There would be no means of _____ possible without a map and working compass.

4. John Harrison became the world's _____ clockmaker.

5. The _____ must be swinging at a constant rate.

C. Choose three words from the box in Part B. Use each word in a sentence.

1. _____

   _____

2. _____

   _____

3. _____

   _____

Build Vocabulary

Visual Clues

conquest	struggling	recovering	survive	calculate	contribution

A. Choose the best answer from the box to complete each sentence.

1. Hector had missed a lot of school and, as a result, was _____ to keep up with his studies.

2. If you _____ the cost of labor and materials you will see how expensive the project is.

3. The roses will not _____ in this cold weather.

4. Jannine's father made a big _____ to the school's baseball team.

5. Pedro spent a week _____ after his surgery.

B. Choose the word from the box that most closely fits each of the following descriptions of an illustration.

1. A well-dressed man, with a group of men standing behind him and watching, hands John Harrison an envelope. _____

2. A man sits with his wife in the kitchen of what looks like a shack. There five children gathered around a very small table eating a small amount of food. _____

3. A mother is feeding soup to an ill-looking boy who is lying in bed. _____

4. John Harrison has a book in front of him and appears to be trying to figure something out. In the background you see what he is thinking about: ships and longitude. _____

5. Harrison and another man are looking at Harrison's wonderfully contructed clocks. The text says that three of his clocks are over 300 years old. _____

C. Choose three words from the box. Use each word in a sentence that is <u>not</u> about John Harrison or his clocks.

1. _____

_____

2. _____

_____

3. _____

_____

Homophones

A. Circle the correct homophone.

1. Which word means "they are"?

   a. they're   **b.** there

2. Which word means "a hard material that comes from trees"?

   a. wood   **b.** would

3. Which word means "to use or have something as clothing"?

   a. wear   **b.** where

4. Which word means "to be tired by things or people that are dull and uninteresting"?

   a. board   **b.** bored

5. Which word means "a portion of an object or material"?

   a. peace   **b.** piece

B. Complete each sentence with the correct homophone.

1. Claire _____ like to go to the mall with you. (wood, would)

2. Amos is still waiting for a _____ of pie. (piece, peace)

3. The _____ decided not to contribute to the inventor's project. (board, bored)

4. _____ did you park the car? (Where, Wear)

5. _____ been three years since Frank has seen his best friend. (Its, It's)

there/their/they're	our/hour	wood/would	board/bored	where/wear	its/it's

C. Choose three homophone sets from the box. Use each word in a sentence.

1. _____

   _____

   _____

2. _____

   _____

   _____

3. _____

   _____

   _____

Compound-Complex Sentences

A. Identify the dependent clause that begins with a <u>subordinate conjunction</u> in each sentence. Circle the correct answer.

1. Until you read the final chapter of the book, you may expect the main character to win, but you would be wrong

   a. Until you read the final chapter of the book   **b.** you may expect the main character to win

2. After Jerome solved the math problem, he moved on to a new challenge, but he could not complete that one.

   a. After Jerome solved the math problem   **b.** he moved on to a new challenge

3. The experiment worked even though we added the wrong amount of liquid, but we could not replicate the process.

   a. The experiment worked   **b.** even though we added the wrong amount of liquid

4. Even though the study was flawed, the scientists were encouraged by the results, so the company gave them more funding.

   a. Even though the study was flawed

   b. the scientists were encouraged by the results

B. Complete each dependent clause.

   1. Even though _____, it grew very large and survived a few nights.

   2. If _____, they will find wealth in the West, but they will have to risk their lives.

   3. Because _____ the travelers risked their lives, and some succeeded.

   4. Although _____, other explorers failed, and their families had to make due.

C. Choose one topic and write three compound-complex sentences about it. Possible topics:

explorers	conducting a science experiment

   1. _____

   2. _____

   3. _____

Write an Argument

To evaluate your argument, use the Written Argument Rubric available from your online Student Resources or from your teacher.

A. Plan Your Argument

1. Think about this question: *Would John Harrison have been better off living as a respected and gifted carpenter?*

After thinking it over, what do you think? **Yes** or **No?**

2. Is your answer based on your personal preferences, or did you consider the time and environment in which Harrison lived? Explain your answer.

_____

_____

_____

_____

_____

_____

_____

3. Take notes on reasons for your claim. Include evidence from the graphic novel.

_____

_____

_____

_____

_____

_____

_____

_____

B. Write Your Argument

Use your Part A notes to write your argument on another sheet of paper. Remember to include the following:

1. an opening statement that states your claim (your answer to the question *Would John Harrison have been better off living as a gifted and respected carpenter?*)

2. reasons for your claim

3. evidence from the selection that supports your claim and your reasons

4. a closing statement that restates your claim

Speak Out! Support

Reread the graphic novel and look closely at every frame that shows members of the Longitude Board. Use the illustrations and the dialogue to figure out what the Longitude Commissioners' attitudes were. Take notes to complete the following chart.

Pages/ Frames	Details I Notice About the Commissioners' Facial Expressions, Clothing, "Body Language," and Dialogue
p. 252 frame 3	_____ _____ _____ _____
p. 252 frame 4	_____ _____ _____ _____
p. 252 frame 5	_____ _____ _____ _____
p. 253 frame 3	_____ _____ _____ _____
p. 253 frame 4	_____ _____ _____ _____

Word Families

| education | difference | mechanism | precise | expanded |

A. Choose a word from the box to answer each question.

1. Which word means "very accurate and exact"? _____

2. Which word means "a piece of a machine or a machine part"? _____

3. Which word means "increased in size or amount"? _____

4. Which word means "the process of receiving knowledge, skills, or understanding"?
_____

B. Complete the sentences with the correct word from the box at the top of the page.

1. I _____ my essay by adding more facts and details.

2. The _____ that controls the heat in the house is broken.

3. Carpenters must take _____ measurements.

4. There is a big _____ between Spanish food and Mexican food.

C. Choose two words from the box at the top of the page and use them in a sentence. Next, use a dictionary to find two words that are from the same word families as the words you chose from the box. Use the two words from the dictionary in the second sentence.

1. _____

_____

_____

_____

2. _____

_____

_____

_____

Topics for a Written Argument

Follow the instructions on page 56 of the Student Book before working on this page.

A. Below are the selections from this unit. Pick three of them and write a claim related to each of your choices.

"The Network Kid"

"Babe Secoli"

"The Village Blacksmith"

"Podcast: Chris Hadfield on the Future of Manned Space Exploration"

"What Work Means"

"Mother Jones and the Children's Crusade"

"John Harrison—Clockmaker"

_____

_____

_____

B. Write three possible topics for your written argument.

Idea 1 _____

_____

_____

Idea 2 _____

_____

_____

Idea 3 _____

_____

_____

Plan Your Written Argument

To evaluate your written argument, use the Written Argument Rubric available from your online Student Resources or from your teacher.

Make a Claim

Write your claim as a statement. Include an interesting fact or question to make readers curious about your topic.

_____

_____

Find Reasons/Know Your Sources

What reasons, facts, and opinions from the selections will support your claim?

Reason/fact/opinion	Unit Selection

What reasons, facts, and opinions from the other sources might you include? (Name credible sources.)

Reason/fact/opinion	Source

Think About Style

What technical or unfamiliar words related to your topic do you need to explain?

_____

_____

_____

_____

Academic Vocabulary

A. Complete each sentence with the correct word from the box.

style	stylish

1. Al looked very modern in his _____ hat.

stylistic	stylistically

2. The two candidates' speeches contained different ideas, but they were very _____ similar.

stylish	stylistic

3. For the final draft of his novel, Mr. Crump only made a few _____ changes.

style	stylistically

4. Tasha tries to write informational text in a direct, uncomplicated _____.

B. Read the passage and answer the questions.

> Elsa is going to meet a young writer in a stylish coffee shop for an interview. Although the writer's new book seems stylistically similar to some other fantasy novels at first, her unique word choices and unusual sentences create a magical style that invites the reader to believe in fantasy.

1. How does the writer's new book seem similar to some other fantasy novels?

It seems _____.

2. What do her unique word choices and unusual sentences create?

They create _____.

3. What is special about the coffee shop where she will meet Elsa?

It is a _____.

C. Using a word from the box, write a sentence about your own style when you write stories or poetry.

style	stylistic	stylistically

_____

_____

Finalize Your Plan

WRITING TOOLBOX

Elements of a Written Argument

Introduction	The *introduction* should make a claim about an issue or a problem that needs to be solved.
Reasons	Provide *reasons* that support your claim. (Facts are best, but opinions can be valuable, too!) Respond to opposing viewpoints with evidence from the text.
Conclusion	The *conclusion* restates your argument and summarizes the evidence. You can also use this section to offer a comment of your own or ask a thought-provoking question.

A. Review the elements of an written argument above. Describe the elements that you will include in your argument.

Introduction _____

_____

_____

Reasons _____

_____

_____

Conclusion _____

_____

_____

B. Write a brief summary of your essay.

_____

_____

_____

_____

Vocabulary Review

Here are some of the words you learned in this unit. Choose words from this list and sort them into the categories below. There are many possible correct answers! Also, many of the words fit into more than one category.

board	effort	mechanism	repose
bored	employment	minority	retirement
brainstormed	enforce	occupy	stylish
brawny	exertion	option	symbolic
comment	exploitation	orbit	textile
discount	fanciful	our	their
displacement	hour	park	they're
distortion	industry	prohibiting	toil
drudgery	infallible	reference	tragedy
education	labor	rejoice	typewriter

Nouns

1. _____
2. _____
3. _____
4. _____

Words with Prefixes

1. _____
2. _____
3. _____
4. _____

Synonyms for "Work"

1. _____
2. _____
3. _____
4. _____

Homophones

1. _____
2. _____
3. _____
4. _____

Easily Confused Words

A. Decide which word best completes the sentence. Circle the correct answer.

1. The medicine may have side _____.

   a. affects   **b.** effects

2. I hope that the rain does not _____ the game.

   a. affect   **b.** effect

3. The _____ is a leader in the school.

   a. principle   **b.** principal

4. The _____ of the country allow for justice.

   a. principles   **b.** principals

B. Fill in the blank with a word that fits.

1. Luna helped the _____ of her school.

2. The researcher studied the _____ of sleep on performance.

3. Don't let the noise _____ your work.

4. The bright lights do _____ my sleep.

5. I must have strong _____ if I want to succeed.

C. Choose one topic and write four sentences about it. Use at least three of the following words: *affect, effect, principal, principle.* Possible topics:

working with the school	medicine	a country

1. _____

   _____

2. _____

   _____

3. _____

   _____

4. _____

   _____